Paul Constance

French in 10 days

Language course with a new method

AF138994

Publishing house:
Books on Demand
Norderstedt, Germany
ISBN 978-3-7322-6259-5
© 2013 Paul Constance
Cover: Sacré-Coeur in Paris
Photo: Paul Constance

Table of contents

First day

Le contrôle douanier / The customs check

Place: The airport Charles de Gaulle in Paris.
tourist T, customs officer O

O Bonjour (bo<u>sh</u>ur). Good afternoon. Le passeport s'il vous plait (loe paspOr silvuplE). The passport please. Le passeport est périmé (E perime). The passport has expired.

T Voici la carte d'identité (vwasi la kart did*a*tite). This is my identity card. J'ai voyagé beaucoup de temps par l'Angleterre (<u>sh</u>e vwaja<u>sh</u>e boku doe t*a* par l*a*gloetEr). I have been travelling for a long time in England. Il y a <u>quelque chose</u> de nouveau en France (ilja kElke <u>shos</u> doe nuvo *a* fr*a*s)? Is there <u>anything</u> new in France?

O Je ne sais pas (<u>sh</u>oe noe sE pa). I don't know. Vous avez quelque chose à déclarer (vu<u>s</u>ave kElke <u>shos</u> a deklare)? Do you have anything to declare?

T Je n'ai rien à déclarer (<u>sh</u>oe ne rj*e* a deklare). I don't have anything to declare.

O Ouvrez cette valise (uvre sEt vali<u>s</u>)! Open this case! Maintenant je sais quelque chose de nouveau pour vous (m*e*tn*a*t <u>sh</u>oe sE kElke <u>shos</u> doe nuvo pur vu). Now I know something new for you. Vous devez payer *les droits de douane* pour ceci (vu doeve peje le drwa doe duan pur soesi)! You have to pay *duty* on this!

T Mais c'est un cadeau (mE sEt*e* kado). But this is a gift.

O Pour qui (pur ki)? For whom ?

T Pour vous (pur vu). For you.

O Je vous remercie (<u>sh</u>oe vu roemErsi). Thank you very much.

T De rien (doe rj*e*). Don't mention it.

The underlined or italic words have the same meaning.

5

Phonetics (PH)

Two rules for the phonetics:
A voiced sound is underlined.
An open vowel is indicated by a capital letter.

	PH	explanation	example	PH	translation
a à	a	like mother	lac	lak	lake
c	k	like come	cabine	kabin	cabin
	s	before e, i, y	cela	soela	that
		voiceless s	ici	isi	here
		like in cell	cycle	sikl	cycle
ç	s	like façade	ça	sa	that
ch	sh	like shoe	chat	sha	cat
é	e	closed high like fiancé	été	ete	summer
	E	open like let	mer	mEr	sea
è	E	open	mère	mEr	mother
ê	E	open	arrêt	arE	stop
g	g	like in garage	gare	gar	station
	<u>sh</u>	before e, i, y like garage	rouge	rou<u>sh</u>	red
			girafe	<u>sh</u>iraf	giraffe
gn	gn	like canyon	agneau	agno	lamb
h		always silent	hôtel	otEl	hotel
j	<u>sh</u>	like déjà vu	jour	<u>sh</u>ur	day
ll	l	like in like	aller	ale	go
	j	like yes	fille	fij	daughter
o	o	closed (shop)	beau	bo	pretty
	O	open like not	pomme	pOm	apple
q(u)	k	like pique	quatre	katr	four
s	s	voiceless (sun)	salle	sal	hall
	<u>s</u>	between vowels	rose	ro<u>s</u>	rose
v	v	like value	verre	vEr	glass

w	w	like whisky	oui	**w**i	yes
y	i	before conso- nant: like see	style	stil	style
	j	like yes	yoga	**j**Oga	yoga
z	s̱	like z in zero	zéro	s̱ero	zero
au	o	o closed	aussi	osi	also
eu	oe	closed (about)	deux	doe	two
	OE	open like hurt	soeur	sOEr	sister
oi	wa	like **foie** gras	oiseau	**wa**so	bird
ou	u	like soup	pour	pur	for

u (phonetics: **y**) does not exist in English. You have to purse up your lips as if you wanted to say oo, but you pronounce ee.

ui	**yi**	short y + i	nuit	ny**i**	night

Nasal sounds

Vowels followed by 'm' or 'n' are usually nasal. A nasal vowel is a sound made by expelling air through the nose; 'm' and 'n' are not pronounced.

Nasal a: PH *a*

a is pronounced like president Mitterrand (miter*a*).

am		lampe	l*a*p	lamp
an		tante	t*a*t	aunt
em		emporter	*a*porte	take away
en		entre	*a*tr	between
ent		lent	l*a*	slow
ment		moment	mom*a*	moment

Nasal a, f. ex. am, an, em, en

7

Nasal e: PH *e*

e is pronounced like president Giscard d'Estaing
(<u>sh</u>iskardEst*e*)

aim	faim	f*e*	hunger
ain	pain	p*e*	bread
eim, ein	sein	s*e*	breast
ien	bien	bj*e*	well
im	impair	*e*pEr	odd
in	vin	v*e*	wine
um, un	parfum	parf*e*	perfume

Nasal e, f. ex. ien, im, in, um, un

Nasal o: PH *o*

o is pronounced like president Pompidou (p*o*pidu)

om	tomber	t*o*be	fall
on	ton	t*o*	tone
tion	station	stasj*o*	station

Nasal o, f. ex. om, on

Rules of the pronunciation

Mostly final consonants are not pronounced, f. ex.
sport (spOr) sport
Before a vowel or a silent h final consonants are
pronounced, f. ex.
les autos (le<u>s</u>oto) the cars
son hôtel (sonotel) his hotel
The final e is not pronounced, f. ex.
rose (ro<u>s</u>) rose
Before a vowel i and y > j, f. ex.
kiosque (kjOsk) kiosk
bruyant (bruj*a*) loud

8

OP <u>Accents</u>

1. The acute accent: only over e   été / summer

2. The grave accent:
   over a   là / there
   over e   mère / mother
   over u   où / where

3. The circumflex accent: gâteau / cake
   over all the vowels   tête / head
        île / island
        dôme / dome
        sûr / sure

<u>French alphabet</u>

How to pronounce the letters of the alphabet in French
when you are spelling a word:
A (a) B (be) C (se) D (de) E (e) F (Ef) G (<u>she</u>)
H (ash) I (i) J (<u>shi</u>) K (ka) L (El) M (Em) N (En) O (o)
P (pe) Q (ky) R (Er) S (Es) T (te) U (y) V (ve)
W (dubloeve) X (iks) Y (i grEk) Z (<u>s</u>Ed)

<u>Abbreviations</u>

derivation of the grammatical rules	D
example	EX
optional part	**OP**
present perfect	Pr Pf
plural	Pl
singular	Sg
phonetics	PH
rule	R

Please learn the underlined words from <u>accident</u> to <u>car</u>.

Second day

Où est la gare? Where is the station?

Place: Paris
tourist T, passer-by P

T Excusez-moi, madame (Ekskysemwa madam). Excuse me, madam. Pourriez-vous me donner quelques informations (purievu moe done kElkeseformasjo)? Could you give me some information? Où est la 'gare de l'est' (u E la gar doe lEst)? Where is the station 'gare de l'est'?

P Au centre de la ville (o satr doe la vil). In the city centre.

T Je peux m'y rendre à pieds (<u>sh</u>oe poe mi radr a pje)? Can I go *there* on foot?

P Ce n'est pas possible, parce que c'est trop loin (soe nE pa pOsibl parskoe sE tro loe). It's not possible because it's too far. La gare est à une distance de dix kilomètres d'ici (la gar Eta yn distas doe di kilOmEtr disi).The station is ten kilometres from here.

T Comment puis-je me rendre à la gare (kOma pyi<u>sh</u>oe moe radr a la gar)? How can I get to the station?

P Vous préférez l'autobus ou le métro (vu prefere lotobys u loe metro)? Do you prefer bus or underground? Tous les deux vont à la gare (tu le doe vot a la gar). Both of them go to the station.

T Ça m'est égal (sa mEt egal). I don't mind. Où se trouve l'arrêt d'autobus ou la station de métro (u soe truv larE dotobys u la stasjo doe metro)? Where is the bus stop or the underground station?

P Là - bas vous voyez l'arrêt d'autobus (laba vu vwaje larE dotobys). There is the bus stop.

T Quel autobus va à la gare (kEl otobys va a la gar)? Which bus goes to the station?

P Vous devez prendre le bus numéro trente (vu doeve pr*a*dr loe bys nymero tr*a*t). You need to get the bus number thirty.

T *Combien* d'arrêts y a-t-il jusqu'à la gare (k*o*bj*e* darE jatil <u>sh</u>ysk a la gar)? *How many* stops are there to the station.

P *Je suis désolée*, je ne le sais pas (<u>sh</u>oe syi desOle <u>sh</u>oe noe loe sE pa). *Sorry*, I don't know.

T Ça ne fait rien (sa noe fE rj*e*), merci (mErsi). It does not matter, thank you.

The definite article

EX   The boy and the girl eat the orange.
     Le garçon e **la** fille (1) mangent **l'**orange (2).

Pl   **Les** garçons et **les** filles mangent **les** oranges (3).

D 1   There are two definite articles:
       le (masculine), **la** (feminine).

   2   Before a vowel or a silent h
       le and la > **l'**.

   3   The plural of le, la, l': **les**
       Before a vowel or a silent h the s is pronounced,
       f. ex: les oranges, les hôtels

OP The definite article and its use

EX   The French love the Seine which goes through France.
     Les français aiment la Seine qui va par la France

D   The definite article is used in front of the names of peoples, countries and rivers.

The contracted definite article

EX   The girl is the boy's friend.
     La fille est l'amie **du** garçon (1).

11

PL   Les filles sont les amies **des** garçons (2).
D   1   **de + le > du**.
    2   **de + les > des**.
EX   The girl gives the orange to the boy.
      La fille donne l'orange **au** garçon (1).
PL   Les filles donnent les oranges **aux** garçons (2).
D   1   **à + le > au**.
    2   **à + les > aux**.
      Exception: The prepositions à and de don't contract
      with **l'**, f. ex.
      Je vais **à l'**hôtel. I go to the hotel.
      Je viens **de l'**hôtel. I come from the hotel.

The partitive article

EX   Do you want beer / voulez-vous **de la** bière? (1)
      I don't want beer / je ne veux pas **de** bière (2)
      I want a glass of wine / je veux un verre **de** vin
      (3)
D   1   **de + the definite article > the partitive article**
      The partitive article is used in front of an
      indeterminate quantity.
      The preposition **de** is used **alone**:
    2   after a verb in the negative
    3   after a determinate quantity

The indefinite article

EX   A boy and a girl eat an orange.
      Un garçon et **une** fille mangent **une** orange (1).
PL   **Des** garçons et **des** filles mangent **des** oranges (2).
D   1   There are two indefinite articles:
      un (m), **une** (f)
    2   The plural of un, une: **des**
      des indicates an indefinite number of something.

Conjugation: avoir / to have and être / to be

present	j'**ai** (1)	je **suis** (2)
présent	tu **as**	tu **es**
1 I have	il / elle **a**	il / elle **est**
2 I am	nous av**ons**	nous **sommes**
	vous av**ez**	vous **êtes**
	ils / elles **ont**	ils / elles **sont**

imperfect	j'av**ais** (1)	j'**étais** (2)
imparfait	tu av**ais**	tu étais
1 I had	il / elle av**ait**	il / elle était
2 I was	nous av**ions**	nous ét**ions**
	vous av**iez**	vous ét**iez**
	ils / elles av**aient**	ils / elles ét**aient**

future	The future has the same endings as the present
futur	of 'avoir'.

1 I will have	j'aur**ai** (1)	je ser**ai** (2)
2 I will be	tu aur**as**	tu ser**as**
	il / elle aur**a**	il / elle ser**a**
	nous aur**ons**	nous ser**ons**
	vous aur**ez**	vous ser**ez**
	ils / elles aur**ont**	ils / elles ser**ont**

conditional	The conditional has the same endings
conditionnel	as the imperfect of 'avoir'.

1 I would have	j'aur**ais** (1)	je ser**ais** (2)
2 I would be	tu aur**ais**	tu ser**ais**
	il / elle aur**ait**	il / elle ser**ait**
	nous aur**ions**	nous ser**ions**
	vous aur**iez**	vous ser**iez**
	ils / elles aur**aient**	ils / elles ser**aient**

13

The cardinal numerals

0 zéro (_s_ero)	100 cent (s_a_)
1 un _(e)_	101 cent un (s_a_ _e_)
2 deux (doe)	200 deux cents (doe s_a_)
3 trois (trwa)	1000 mille (mil)
4 quatre (katr)	1000000 un million
5 cinq (s_e_k)	(_e_ milj_o_)
6 six (sis)	
7 sept (s_E_t)	
8 huit (yit)	
9 neuf (n_OE_f)	
10 dix (dis)	
11 onze (_o_s̲)	
12 douze (du_s̲_)	
13 treize (tr_E_s̲)	
14 quatorze (kat_O_rs̲)	
15 quinze (k_e_s̲)	
16 seize (s_E_s̲)	
17 dix-sept (dis_E_t)	
18 dix-huit (disyit)	
19 dix-neuf (disn_OE_f)	
20 vingt (v_e_)	
21 vingt-et-un (v_e_te _e_)	
22 vingt-deux (v_e_doe)	
30 trente (tr_a_t)	
40 quarante (kar_a_t)	
50 cinquante (s_e_k_a_t)	
60 soixante (swas_a_t)	
70 soixante-dix (swas_a_t dis)	
71 soixante et onze (swas_a_t e _o_s̲)	
72 soixante-douze (swas_a_t du_s̲_)	
80 quatre-vingt (katroe v_e_)	
81 quatre-vingt-un (katroe v_e_ _e_)	
90 quatre-vingt-dix (katroe v_e_ dis)	

The ordinal numerals and the fractions

The ordinal numeral is formed like this: the cardinal
numeral + -ième (PH: jEm). Exception: premier, première.

first	premier (m), première (f)
second	deuxième (doesjEm)
third	troisième 1/3: un tiers
fourth	quatrième 1/4: un quart
fifth	cinquième 1/5: un cinquième
sixth	sixième (sisjEm)
seventh	septième (sEtjEm)
eighth	huitième (yitjEm)
ninth	neuvième (noevjEm)
tenth	dixième 1/10: un dixième

What's the date

On est le combien aujourd´hui? What's the date today?
Nous sommes le premier mai; le trois mai je vais à Paris.
Today is the first May; the third May I go to Paris.
D For the first day of month is used the ordinal number, for
the other days the cardinal numbers.

What time is it?

Quelle heure est - il (kEl OEr Et il)? What time is it?

	Il est
1.00	une heure
1.15	une heure quinze
1.30	une heure trente
1.45	une heure quarante cinq
2.00	deux heures

Please learn the underlined words from <u>carry</u> to <u>cup</u>.

Third day

La grève / The strike

Place: Station in Marseille
tourist T, employee E

T (devant le guichet / in front of the ticket office):
À quelle heure est le prochain train pour Paris (a kEl OEr E loe prOsh*e* tr*e* pur pari)? *What time* is the next train to Paris?

E Je ne le sais pas (<u>sh</u>oe noe loe sE pa). I don't know. *Depuis hier*, au lieu de l'horaire, nous avons une grève (doepyi ijEr o ljoe doe lOrEr nu<u>s</u>av*o* yn grEv). Instead of the time table we have been on strike *since yesterday*.

T *De quel quai* part le train (doe kEl kE par loe tr*e*) ? *Which platform* does the train leave *from*?

E Du quai six (dy kE sis). From platform six.

T Est-ce que je dois changer de trains (Eskoe <u>sh</u>oe dwa sh*a*<u>sh</u>e doe tr*e*)? Do I have to change trains?

E Oui, vous devez changer de train à Lyon. Yes, you have to change trains at Lyon.

T Je prendrai ma correspondance pour Paris (<u>sh</u>oe pr*a*dre ma kOresp*o*d*a*s pur pari)? Will I have my connection to Paris?

E Certainement non (sErtEnm*a* n*o*). Certainly not.

T *Combien de temps* dure le voyage (k*o*bj*e* doe t*a* dyr loe vwaja<u>sh</u>)? *How long* does the journey last?

E Normalement cinq heures, mais aujourd'hui, par suite de la grève, huit heures (nOrmalm*a* s*e*k Oer mE<u>s</u>o-<u>sh</u>urdyi par syit doe la grEv yit OEr). Normally five hours, but today because of the strike eight.

T Il y a un wagon couchettes (ilja *e* vag*o* kush*Et*)? Is there a couchette?

E Oui, mais par suite de la grève seulement jusqu'à Lyon

16

(wi mE par syit doe la grEv sOElma <u>sh</u>yska lj*o*). Yes, but because of the strike only until Lyon.

T   *Je voudrais* réserver un coin fenêtre et une couchette (<u>sh</u>oe vudrE re<u>s</u>Erve *e* ko*e* foenEtr e yn kushEt). *I would like* to reserve a window seat and a couchette. S'il vous plait un billet en deuxième classe, aller - retour, le retour sans grève (silvuplE *e* bijE *a* doesjEm klas ale roetur loe roetur s*a* grEv). Please give me a second-class return ticket, the return journey without the strike.

The noun

EX   un ami / a boyfriend   une ami**e** / a girlfriend
D   masculine noun + **e** > feminine noun
      Exceptions, f. ex.

vend**eur**	vend**euse**	seller
direc**teur**	direc**trice**	director, directress
écolier	écoli**ère**	schoolboy, schoolgirl

R   The e of the feminine noun is not pronounced.

OP Masculine and feminine nouns

EX   During the journey Paul reads in the newspaper the article: The work of the tourist office.
      Pendant le voy**age** Paul lit dans le journ**al** l'article:
      Le trav**ail** du bureau de tour**isme**.
D   Masculine noun suffixes:
      -age, -al, -ail, -isme.
EX   The break with a baguette and a walk is important for the health.
      La récréa**tion** avec une bague**tte** et une promen**ade** est importante pour la san**té**.
D   Feminine noun suffixes:
      -tion, -ette, -ade, -té.

EX   A ship which transports Renaults goes on the Seine
        through France.
        Un navire qui transporte des Renault va sur la Seine
        par la France.

D   The following nouns are mostly feminine:
        The names of cars and the names of rivers and
        countries with the ending -**e**.

The plural

EX   The boy and the girl eat the orange.
        Le garçon et la fille mangent l'orange.

Pl   Les garçons et les filles mangent les oranges.

D   The plural is made by adding an -**s** to the singular;
        this **s** is not pronounced.

OP The same plural and singular

The nouns in -s, -x, -z have the same Sg and Pl, f. ex.
the arm / le bras Pl les bras
the voice / la voix Pl les voix
the nose / le nez Pl les nez

OP The irregular plural

EX   The child loves the cake and the play.
        L'enfant aime le gâte**au** et le j**eu**.

Pl   Les enfants aiment les gâteaux et les jeux.

D   Nouns ending in -au and -eu have -**x** in the plural.

R   Nouns ending in -al have -**aux** in the plural, f. ex.
        le journal / les journ**aux**

Weekdays

Monday	lundi l*e*di
Tuesday	mardi
Wednesday	mercredi mErkroedi
Thursday	jeudi <u>sh</u>oedi
Friday	vendredi v*a*droedi
Saturday	samedi samdi
Sunday	dimanche dim*a*sh

Months

January	janvier <u>sh*a*</u>vje
February	février fevrije
March	mars
April	avril
May	mai mE
June	juin <u>sh</u>yi*e*
July	juillet <u>sh</u>yijE
August	août u(t)
September	septembre sEpt*a*br
October	octobre OktObr
November	novembre nov*a*br
December	décembre des*a*br

Seasons

spring	printemps pr*eta*
summer	été
autumn	automne otOn
winter	hiver ivEr

R Weekdays, months and seasons are **masculine**.

Please learn the underlined words from <u>cut</u> to <u>flower**</u>.**

Fourth day

La panne / The breakdown

Place: Paris
tourist T, passer-by P, employee E, mechanic M

T Excusez-moi, où se trouve le garage le plus proche (Ekskysemwa u soe truv loe garash loe ply prOsh)? Excuse me, where is the nearest garage?

P (en riant / smiling) Cinq mètres derrière vous (sek mEtr dErjEr vu). Five meters behind you.

E Bonjour, qu'est-ce qu'il y a (boshur kEskilja)? Hello, what's the matter ?

T Ma voiture est en panne (ma vwatyr Eta pan). My car has broken down. Pourriez-vous vérifier ma voiture (purievu verifie ma vwatyr)? Could you check my car? Elle s'est arrêté et ne démarre plus (El sEtarEte e noe demar ply). It has just stopped and won't start again.

E Où s'est-elle arrêtée (u sEtEl arEte)? Where has it stopped?

T Exactement devant le garage (Egsaktoema doeva loe garash). Exactly in front of the garage.

E Bravo, c'est une bonne voiture (bravo sEtyn bOn vwatyr). Well done, it's a good car. S'il vous plaît la clef de la voiture (silvuplE la kle doe la vwatyr). Please give me the car key. Pendant que mon mécanicien contrôle la voiture, vous pouvez boire un café (pada koe mo mekanisje kotrol la vwatyr vu puve bwar e kafe). While my mechanic checks the car you can drink a coffee.

Le mécanicien retourne dans 5 minutes. The mechanic returns after 5 minutes.

T Pourquoi la voiture ne démarre plus (purkwa la vwatyr noe demar ply)? Why does the car not start?

M Devinez un peu (doevine e poe). Have a guess.

20

T   Le démarreur ne fonctionne pas (loe demarOEr noe
    f*o*ksjOn pa)? The starter doesn't work?
M   Non (n*o*). No.
T   La batterie est à plat (la batri Eta pla)? Is the battery
    flat?
M   Non, mais le réservoir d'essence est vide (n*o* mE loe
    resErvwar des*a*s E vid). No, but the tank is empty.

Adjectives

EX The little boy and the little girl eat the orange.
    Le petit garçon et la petite fille (1) mangent l'orange.
Pl Les petits garçons et les petites filles (2) mangent
    les oranges.
D 1 The masculine form (petit) + **e** > the feminine form
    (petite).
    If the masculine form ends in an -e the adjective
    doesn't change in the feminine, f. ex.
    le jeune garçon, la jeune fille.
  2 The singular form (petite) + **s** > the plural form
    (petites)
R   Adjectives agree in number and gender with the noun
    to which they refer.

OP

When the nouns are of different gender, the adjective goes
into the masculine plural, f. ex. Les garçons et les filles sont
gentils / the boys and the girls are nice.

OP Adjectives with two masculine singulars

m	m	f	
beau	bel	belle	beautiful
nouveau	nouvel	nouvelle	new
vieux	vieil	vieille	old

The 2nd masculine Sg is used before a vowel or a silent h,
f. ex. un bel enfant / a good looking child

Position of the adjective

EX The French captain has a red ship with a big sail and
    a second electric motor.
    Le capitaine français (1) a un bateau rouge (2)
    avec une grande voile (3) et un deuxième (4) moteur
    électrique.

D   The adjectives are mostly placed after the noun.
    Always are placed after the noun:
    adjectives which express the nationality (1) the
    colour (2) or the form.
    Before the noun are placed:
    short adjectives (3) and numerals (4).

The comparative and the superlative

A is beautiful / A est **belle**
B is more beautiful than A / B est **plus belle** que A
C is the most beautiful / C est **la plus belle**
D is less beautiful than A / D est **moins belle** que A
D is the least beautiful / D est **la moins belle**.

D   The comparative of superiority: plus + adjective
    The comparative of inferiority: moins + adjective
    The superlative is formed by adding the definite article
    before the comparative.

To introduce oneself

Place : Paris
Persons: Ms H … Mr C …

C· How are you? Comment allez-vous (kOm*a*tale vu)?
H   Fine thanks and you? Très bien, merci, et vous (trE bj*e*
    mErsi, e vu)?
C   My name is Cock. Je m'appelle Cock (shoe mapEl).

What is your name? Comment vous appelez-vous (kOm*a* vu*s*aple vu)?

H My name is Hen. Je m'appelle Hen.

C Pleased to meet you. Enchanté (*e*sh*a*te). *Where* are you *from*? Vous êtes *d'où* (vu*s*Et du)?

H I am from Britain. Je viens de la Grande-Bretagne (<u>sh</u>oe vi*a* doe la gr*a*dbroetagn).

C My ancestors are from Britain too. Mes ancêtres sont venus de la Grande-Bretagne aussi (mes*a*sEtr s*o* voeny doe la gr*a*dbroetagn osi).

H ... I am sorry, I have to go now. Je suis désolée, je dois maintenant partir (<u>sh</u>oe syi desOle <u>sh</u>oe dwa m*e*tn*a* partir). It was nice meeting you, Mr Cock. Ravie d'avoir fait votre connaissance, monsieur Cock (ravi davwar fE vOtr kOnEs*a*s moesjoe).

C Goodbye Ms Hen, have a good return to Britain. Au revoir, madame Hen, bon retour en Grande Bretagne (o roevwar madam b*o* roetur).

Irregular verbs

aller / go
pres. je vais, tu vas, il/elle va, nous allons, vous allez, ils/elles vont
Pr Pf je suis allé
faire / do
pres. je fais, nous faisons, vous faites, ils/elles font
Pr Pf j'ai fait
pouvoir / can
pres. je peux, nous pouvons, ils/elles peuvent
Pr Pf j'ai pu
voir / see
pres. je vois, nous voyons, ils/elles voient
Pr Pf j'ai vu
Please learn the underlined words from <u>follow</u> to <u>hotel</u>.

Fifth day

Première rencontre / First meeting

Place: Market square in Capri. In front of a hotel. Beside
the entrance: two suitcases.
female tourist F, male tourist M

M Ça vous plait ici (sa vu plE isi)? Do you like it here?

F Oui, ça me plait très bien (wi sa moe plE trE bj*e)*. Yes,
I like it very much.

M Où habitez-vous (u abitevu)? Where do you live?

F J'habite à Rome (<u>sh</u>abit a rOm). I live in Rome.

M Quelle surprise, moi aussi (kEl syrpri<u>s</u> mwa osi). What a
surprise, me too. Je m'appelle Tino Baci (<u>sh</u>oe mapEl).
I am Tino Baci.

F (en souriant / smiling) Enchantée (*a*sha*t*e). Pleased to
meet you.

M Comment vous appelez-vous (kOm*a* vu<u>s</u>aplevu)? What
is your name?

F Je m'appelle Gina Borelli (<u>sh</u>oe mapEl). I am Gina
Borelli.

M Avez-vous trouvé un bon hôtel (avevu truve *e* b*o*notEl)?
Did you find a good hotel?

F Oui, cet hôtel là (wi sEtotEl). Yes, the hotel there.

M Quelle surprise, je suis aussi dans cet hôtel (kEl syrpri<u>s</u>
<u>sh</u>oe syi osi d*a* sEtotEl). What a surprise, I am also in
this hotel. C'est la première fois que vous êtes ici?
(sE la proemiEr fwa koe vu<u>s</u>Et isi)? Is this your first
time here?

F Oui, c'est la première fois (wi sE la proemiEr fwa). Yes,
this is the first time I have been here.

M Vous êtes ici avec la famille (vu<u>s</u>Et isi avEk la famij)?
Are you here with your family?

F Non, je suis seule (n*o* <u>sh</u>oe syi sOEl). No, I am alone.

24

M Moi aussi (mwa osi). Me too. Je suis arrivé hier (shoe syisarive ijEr). I arrived yesterday. Quand êtes-vous arrivée (ka Etvusarive)? When did you get here?

F Il y a une semaine (ilja yn soemEn). A week ago today.

M Vous êtes ici pour *combien de temps* (vusEt isi pur kobje doe ta)? *How long* are you staying?

F Je suis en train de partir (shoe syisa tre doe partir). I am just leaving. Voilà mes valises (vwala me valis). There are my cases. J'attends le chauffeur de taxi pour aller au port (shata loe shofOEr doe taksi pur ale o pOr). I am waiting for the taxi driver in order to go to the port.

M Quel dommage (kEl domash)! What a pity! Est-ce qu'on peut se revoir à Rome (Esko poe soe roevwar a rOm)? Can we see each other in Rome? Nous allons au cinéma (nusalo o sinema)? Would you like to go to the cinema?

F Je ne m'intéresse pas au cinéma (shoe noe meterEs pa o sinema). I am not interested in the cinema.

M Nous allons à une discothèque (nusalo a yn diskOtEk)? Would you like to go to a discotheque?

F Je n'ai pas envie d'aller à une discothèque (shoe ne pasevi dale a yn diskOtEk). I don't want to go to a discotheque.

M De quoi vous occupez-vous dans votre temps libre (doe kwa vusokypevu da vOtr ta libr)? What do you do in your spare time?

F Mon hobby est l'opéra (monobi E lOpera). My hobby is the opera.

M C'est aussi mon hobby (sEtosi monobi). That is also my hobby. Vous avez du temps le six septembre (vusave dy ta loe sis sEptabr)? Are you free on the sixth of September?

F Un moment, s'il vous plait (*e* moma silvuplE). Just a moment, please. Je dois regarder mon agenda (shoe dwa roegarde monasheda). I will have a look in my diary. Oui, le six septembre je suis libre (wi loe sis sEptabr

25

<u>sh</u>oe syi libr). Yes, the sixth September is free.

M (prend son téléphone portable et compose un numéro de téléphone / takes his mobile and dials a phone number):

Qu'est-ce qu'il y a le six septembre à l'opéra (kEskilja loe sis sEpt*a*br a lOpera)? What is on the sixth of September at the opera? Oh, une première (yn proemjEr). Oh, a premiere. Qui est le soliste (ki E loe sOlist)? Who is the soloist? Oh, Placido Domingo. Il y a encore deux places (ilja *a*kOr doe plas)? Are there still two seats? Je voudrais réserver deux places au balcon (<u>sh</u>oe vudrE re<u>s</u>Erve doe plas o balk*o*). I would like to reserve two seats in the gallery.

F Qu'est-ce qu'il y a à l'opéra (kEskilja a lOpera) ? What is on at the opera?

M (en souriant / smiling): Le mariage du Figaro (loe mar-ja<u>sh</u> dy figaro). The Figaro's marriage.

Adverbs

EX The slow boy eats slowly.
 Le lent garçon mange lentement.
D The feminine form of the adjective (lente) + ment > the adverb (lentement).

Adjectives ending in a vowel: The masculine form of the adjective + ment > the adverbe,

f. ex. vrai + ment > vraiment (really)

R The adverb is invariable.

OP Comparative and superlative of the adverb

A often puts on lipstick / A se maquille **souvent**.

B se maquille **plus souvent** que A

C se maquille **le plus souvent**

D se maquille **moins souvent** que A.

D se maquille **le moins souvent**.

OP Comparative of equality

Charles has just as much risk for health as Paul because he smokes just as much as Paul, he eats just as often as Paul and he is just as fat as Paul.

Charles a **autant de** risque sanitaire **que** Paul (1), parce qu'il fume **autant que** Paul (2), parce qu'il mange **aussi** souvent **que** Paul (3) et parce qu'il est **aussi** gros **que** Paul (4).

D 1 noun: **autant de ... que**

  . 2 verb: **autant que**

 3+4 adverb or adjective: **aussi ... que**

Irregular comparatives and superlatives

EX   After a good dinner I feel well.

        Après un **bon** dîner je me sens **bien**.

        bon (adjective) bien (adverb)

        After a bad diner I feel badly.

        Après un **mauvais** dîner je me sens **mal**.

        mauvais (adjective) mal (adverb)

OP			
	bon	meilleur	le, la meilleur(e)
	good	better	best
	bien	mieux	le mieux
	well	better	best
	mauvais	pire	le, la pire
	bad	worse	worst
	mal	pis	le pis
	badly	worse	worst

OP The two meanings of the word 'on'

EX   **On** doit apprendre / **one** must learn

        On cherche une table / **we** are looking for a table

Contrasting adjectives and adverbs

old / young âgé / jeune; cheap / expensive bon marché / cher; broad / narrow large / étroit; outside / inside dehors / dedans; first / last premier / dernier; free/ occupied libre / occupé; early / late tôt / tard; big / small grand / petit; hard / soft dur / mou; light / dark clair / sombre; warm / cold chaud / froid; here / there ici / là; high / low haut / bas; up / down en haut / en bas; behind / in front derrière / devant; easy / difficult facile / difficile; light / heavy léger / lourd; long / short long / court; on the right / on the left à droite / à gauche; loud / quiet bruyant / silencieux; after / before après / avant; near / distant proche / lointain; above / under dessus / dessous; open / closed ouvert / fermé; right / wrong juste / faux; quick / slow rapide / lent; beautiful / ugly beau / laid; strong / weak fort / faible; sweet / sour doux / acide; full / empty plein / vide.

OP Irregular verbs

boire / drink
pres. je bois, nous buvons, ils/elles boivent
Pr Pf j'ai bu

devoir / have to
pres. je dois, nous devons, ils/elles doivent
Pr Pf j'ai dû

plaire / please
pres. je plais, nous plaisons, ils/elles plaisent
Pr Pf j'ai plu

savoir / know
pres. je sais, nous savons, ils/elles savent
Pr Pf j'ai su

OP At the doctor's

There is a doctor / a pharmacy around here? Il y a une pharmacie / un médecin au voisinage (ilja yn farmasi *e* mEds*e* o vwa<u>s</u>ina<u>sh</u>)?

I am ...	Je suis ...
allergic to	allergique à (alEr<u>sh</u>ik)
vaccinated against	vacciné contre (vaksine k*o*tr)
I have faint	je me suis évanoui (<u>sh</u>oe moe syi evanui)
I have had a fall	tombé (t*o*be)
.. months pregnant	enceinte de .. mois (*a*s*e*t doe ... mwa)
diabetic	diabétique (diabetik)
I have ...	**J'ai ...**
a headache	mal à la tête (mal a la tEt)
an earache	mal aux oreilles (o<u>s</u>orEj)
a sore throat	mal à la gorge (gOr<u>sh</u>)
backache	mal au dos (do)
got an upset stomach	maux d'estomac (mo dEst*O*ma)
stomach ache	mal au ventre (v*a*tr)
a cold	un refroidissement (roefrwadism*a*)
a temperature	de la fièvre (fiEvr)
a cough	la toux (tu)
an indigestion	une indigestion (*e*di<u>sh</u>Estj*o*)
diarrhoea	la diarrhée (diare)
been sick	eu des vomissements (y de vOmism*a*)
high/low blood pressure	une tension élevée/basse (t*a*sj*o*)
a stiff neck	un torticolis (tOrtikOli)
a nausea	la nausée (nose)
circulatory trouble	troubles circulatoires (trubl sirkylatwar)
it hurts here	j'ai mal ici (she mal isi)

I take this medication regularly. Je prends ces médicaments régulièrement (<u>sh</u>oe pr*a* se medikam*a* regyljErm*a*)

Please learn the words from <u>hour</u> to <u>light</u>.

Sixth day

La robe de mariée / The wedding dress

Place: Department store in Rome
Gina G, sales assistant A

A Je peux vous aider (<u>sh</u>oe poe vu<u>s</u>ede)? Can I help you?

G Je cherche une robe de mariée (<u>sh</u>oe shErsh yn rOb doe marie). I am looking for a wedding dress.

A Quelle taille (kEl taj)? What size are you?

G Je porte du 40 (shoe pOrt dy kar*a*t). I am size 40.

A Vous pouvez décrire la robe que vous désirez (vu puve dekrir la rOb koe vu desire)? Could you describe the wedding dress you want to have?

G Je désire une robe élégante et traditionnelle (<u>sh</u>oe desir yn rOb eleg*a*t e tradisjOnEl). I want to have an elegant and traditional dress.

A De quelle couleur (doe kEl kulOEr)? Which colour?

G Je voudrais quelque chose en blanc, mais plus beige que blanc (<u>sh</u>oe vudrE kElkoe <u>sh</u>os*a* bl*a* mE ply bE<u>sh</u> koe bl*a*). I want something in white but more beige than white.

A Celle-ci est élégante et traditionnelle (sElsi Eteleg*a*t e tradisjOnEl). This is elegant and traditional.

G Je peux l'essayer (<u>sh</u>oe poe leseje)? Can I try it on?

A Volontiers (vOl*o*tje). Of course. Voici les cabines d'essayage (vwasi le cabin desEja<u>sh</u>). There are the changing rooms.

G (est debout devant le miroir et regarde heureuse son re-flet / stands in front of the mirror and looks happily at her reflection): Ça va très bien (sa va trE bj*e*)! It fits nicely! Comme c'est beau (kOm sE bo). What a beautiful dress. Cette robe est un rêve (sEt rOb Et*e* rEv). This wedding dress is a dream. Combien coûte ce rêve (k*o*bj*e* kut soe rEv)? How much is this dream?

A Deux mille Euro (doe mil oero). Two thousand Euro.

G Quel dommage (kEl dOma<u>sh</u>). What a pity. Je ne peux pas dépenser plus de mille Euro (<u>sh</u>oe noe poe pa dep*a*se ply doe mil oero). I cannot pay more than a thousand Euro.

A Une minute, s'il vous plait (yn minyt silvuplE); je télé-phone au chef de rayon (<u>sh</u>oe telefOne o shEf doe rEj*o*). Just a minute please; I will speak to the head of department on the phone.

Après le coup de téléphone. After the phone call.

Vous pouvez réaliser le rêve avec mille cinq cent Euro (vu puve reali<u>s</u>e loe rEv avEk mil s*e*k s*a* oero). You can realize your dream with one thousand and five hundred Euro.

G D'accord, je la prends (dakOr <u>sh</u>oe la pr*a*). Okay, I will take it.

Conjugations

First group: Verbs with the infinitive ending -**er**
f. ex. parl**er** / speak

je parl **e** I speak	nous parl ons
tu parl **es**	vous parl ez
il/elle parl **e**	ils/elles parl ent (1)

1 The ending -ent is not pronounced

Second group: Verbs with the infinitive ending -**ir**
f. ex . fin**ir** / finish

je fini **s** I finish	nous fin **iss** ons (1)
tu fini **s**	vous fin **iss** ez
il/elle fini **t**	ils/elles fin **iss** ent

1 Between the radical and the ending: **iss**

31

Third group: Verbs with the infinitive ending -re

f. ex. vend**re** / sell

je vend **s** I sell	nous vend ons
tu vend **s**	vous vend ez
il /elle ven **d**	ils/elles vend ent

R All 3 groups have the same endings in the plural.

Imperfect

The imperfect is formed like this:
The 1st person Pl (present) without the ending + the same endings as the imperfect of the verb 'avoir'.

nous **parl** ons	+	j'av **ais**	>	je parl **ais**
nous **vend** ons	+	j'av **ais**	>	je vend **ais**
nous **finiss** ons	+	j'av **ais**	>	je finiss **ais**
		tu av **ais**	>	tu finiss **ais**
		il av **ait**	>	il finiss **ait**
		nous av **ions**	>	nous finiss **ions**
		vous av **iez**	>	vous finiss **iez**
		ils av **aient**	>	ils finiss **aient**

Conditional

The conditional is formed like this:
Infinitive + the same endings as the imperfect of the verb 'avoir'.

parler	+	j'av **ais**	>	je parler **ais**
vendre	+	j'av **ais**	>	je vendr **ais**
finir	+	j'av **ais**	>	je finir **ais**
		tu av **ais**	>	tu finir **ais**
		il av **ait**	>	il finir **ait**
		nous av **ions**	>	nous finir **ions**
		vous av **iez**	>	vous finir **iez**
		ils av **aient**	>	ils finir **aient**

Future

The future is formed like this:
Infinitive + the same endings as the present of the verb 'avoir'.

parler	+	j'**ai**	>	je parler **ai**
vendre	+	j'**ai**	>	je vendr ai (1)
finir	+	j'**ai**	>	je finir **ai**
		tu **as**	>	tu finir **as**
		il **a**	>	il finir **a**
	nous av **ons**		>	nous finir **ons**
	vous av **ez**		>	vous finir **ez**
		ils **ont**	>	ils finir **ont**

1 The e is leaved out

There is an other form of future which is formed like this:
the present of the verb aller / go + infinitive, f. ex.
je vais partir / I am going to leave

The present perfect

EX   I have waited a nice day. I have started at 8 o'clock. I
        have walked in the country.
        J'ai attendu un beau jour. Je suis parti à 8 heures.
        J'ai marché à la campagne.

verb	infinitive ending	past participle
wait / attendre	-re	**-u**
start / partir	-ir	**-i**
walk / marcher	-er	**-é**

The present perfect is formed like this:
present of avoir / to have or être / to be + past participle

Past participle conjugated with être

EX The boy has returned. The girl has returned.
    Le garçon est rentré. La fille est rentrée.
Pl Les garçons sont rentrés. Les filles sont rentrées.
D   The past participle conjugated with être agrees in
    gender and number with the subject of the verb.

OP The following verbs use the present perfect with être:
    Reflexive verbs and some verbs which express a
    movement, f. ex. aller / go, arriver / arrive, descendre
    / descend, entrer /go in, monter / go upstairs, partir /
    start, retourner / return, sortir / go out, tomber / fall,
    venir / come.

Past participle conjugated with avoir

EX The boy has eaten. The girl has eaten.
    Le garçon a mangé. La fille a mangé.
Pl Les garçons ont mangé. Les filles ont mangé.
D   The past participle conjugated with avoir remains
    invariable.

OP Exception: The past participle agrees in gender and
    number with the proceeding direct object.
EX Did you see the boy / the girl? I have seen him / her.
    Tu as vu le garçon? Je l'ai vu.
    Tu as vu la fille? Je l'ai vue.
Pl Tu as vu les garçons? Je les ai vus.
    Tu as vu les filles? Je les ai vues.

OP The following verbs use the present perfect with
    avoir:
    être: J'ai été / I have been, avoir: J'ai eu / I have had,
    the impersonal verbs: il a neigé / it has snowed
    transitive verbs: Paul a écrit une lettre / Paul has
    written a letter

OP The imperative

R   The imperative is derived of the present

present	imperative
tu parl**es**	parl**e** (**es > e**) / speak!
nous parlons	parlons / let's speak!
vous parlez	parlez / speak!

OP Irregular verbs

mettre / put
pres. je mets, nous mettons, ils/elles mettent
Pr Pf j'ai mis
prendre / take
pres. je prends, nous prenons, ils/elles prennent
Pr Pf   j'ai pris

OP False friends

False friends are *French words* and *English words* that appear to be the same in French and in English, but have a different meaning.

fortuné	wealthy	*fortunate*	heureux
habit m	clothes	*habit*	habitude f
confection f	making	*confection*	sucrerie f
déception f	disappointment	*deception*	tromperie
gentil	nice	*gentle*	doux
sympathique	nice	*sympathetic*	complaisant
actuellement	currently	*actually*	réellement
avertissement	warning	*advertisement*	réclame f
blesser	hurt	*bless*	bénir

Please learn the words from <u>liqueur</u> to <u>party</u>.

Seventh day

Le voyage de noces / The honeymoon

Place: The airport Ciampino in Rome.
Gina G, Tino T, employee E

T À quelle heure le vol charter part pour Paris (a kEl OEr loe vOl shartEr par pur pari)? When does the charter plane leave for Paris?

E Vous avez encore un peu de temps (vu<u>s</u>ave *a*kOr *e* poe doe *ta*). You have still a little time. Le départ est à neuf heures (loe depar Eta noef OEr). The take-off is at nine o'clock.

G À quelle heure arrive l'avion à Paris (a kEl OEr ariv lav-j*o* a pari)? What time does the plane get to Paris?

E Si le décollage est *à l'heure*, l'atterrissage est à onze heures (si loe dekOla<u>sh</u> E a lOEr laterisa<u>sh</u> E a *o*s OEr). If the take-off is *on time,* the landing is at eleven. C'est la première fois que vous allez à Paris (sE la proemjEr fwa koe vu<u>s</u>ale a pari)? Are you going to Paris for the first time?

G Oui, c'est notre voyage de noces (wi sE nOtr vwaja<u>sh</u> doe nOs). Yes, it's our honeymoon.

E Félicitations pour le mariage (felisitasj*o* pur loe marja<u>sh</u>). Congratulations on your marriage. Vous avez trouvé un bon hôtel (vu<u>s</u>ave truve *e* b*o*notEl)? Did you find a good hotel?

T Oui, près de la cathédrale *Notre Dame* au *Quartier Latin* (wi prE doe la katedral notr dam o kartje lat*e*). Yes, nearby the cathedral *Notre-Dame* in the *Quartier latin*.

E J'ai vécu dans ce quartier de 1988 à 1996 (<u>sh</u>e veky d*a* soe kartje). I lived in this district of Paris from 1988 to 1996. Chaque fois que je pense à Paris j'éprouve une grande nostalgie de cette ville merveilleuse (shak fwa

koe shoe pas a pari shepruv yn grad nOstalshi doe sEt
vil mErvEjoes). Each time when I remember Paris I am
homesick for that wonderful city.

G Qu'est-ce qui vous a impressionné le plus à Paris (kEski
vusa eprEsjOne loe ply a pari)? What impressed you
most of all in Paris?

E C'est une demande difficile (sEtyn doemad difisil). It's
a difficult question. Peut-être la vue sur la *Seine* sous les
ponts de Paris ou bien la vue de mon appartement sur le
ciel bleu au-dessus des toits de Paris (poetEtr la vy syr la
sEn su le po doe pari u bje la vy doe monapartma syr loe
sjEl bloe o doesy de twa doe pari). Perhaps the view of
the *Seine* under the bridges of Paris or the view from my
apartment of the blue sky over the roofs of Paris. Peut-
être ce soir-là sur la place de la concorde, quand le
soleil rouge se couchait derrière la tour Eiffel (poetEtr
soe swar la syr la plas de la kokOrd ka loe sOlEj rush
soe kushE dErjEr la tur EfEl). Perhaps that evening on
place Concorde, when the red sun was setting behind the
Eiffel tower. Peut-être cette nuit-là, quand j'ai regardé
l'océan de lumières de la ville du restaurant le plus haut
de la tour Eiffel (poetEtr sEt nyi la ka she roegarde
lOsea doe lymjEr doe la vil dy rEstOra loe ply o doe la
tur EfEl). Perhaps that night, when I looked at the light
of the city from the highest restaurant of the Eiffel tower.
Peut-être la beauté séduisante des danseuses du *Lido* et
du *Moulin Rouge* (poetEtr la bote sedyisat de dasOEs dy
lido e dy mule rush). Perhaps the seductive beauty of the
dancers in the *Lido* and the *Moulin Rouge*. Peut-être ce
matin-là, quand j'ai vu devant l'église *Sacré-Cœur* après
une nuit blanche le lever du soleil rosé (poetEtr soe mate
la ka she vy doeva leglis sakre kOEr aprEsyn nyi blash
loe loeve dy sOlEj rose). Perhaps that morning after a
sleepless night in front of the church *Sacré-Coeur*, when
I looked at the rosy light of the sunrise. Qu'est-ce qui

m'a impressionné le plus (kEski ma eprEsjOne loe ply)?
What impressed me mostly? Je ne le sais pas (<u>sh</u>oe noe
loe sE pa). I don't know. Mais je sais que vous serez très
heureux pendant ce voyage de noces, parce que Paris est
la ville parfaite pour s'aimer et pour cela le lieu idéal
pour un voyage de noces (mE <u>sh</u>oe sE koe vu sere trEs-
oeroe p*ada* soe vwaja<u>sh</u> doe nOs parskoe pari E la vil
parfEt pur seme e pur sela loe ljoe ideal pur *e* vwaja<u>sh</u>
doe nOs). But I know, that you will be very happy during
your honeymoon because Paris is the perfect city for love and therefore the ideal place for a honeymoon. Combien de temps restez-vous à Paris? (k*o*bj*e* doe t*a* rEste
vu a pari)? How long are you staying in Paris?

T Deux semaines (doe soemEn). Two weeks.

G Peut-être aussi quelques jours de plus (poetEtr osi
kElkoe <u>sh</u>ur doe ply). Perhaps also some days moreover.

E Saluez Paris de ma part (salye pari doe ma par). Say
hello to Paris for me. Bonne lune de miel (bOn lyn doe
mjEl). Have a happy honeymoon!

The pronoun

The pronoun replaces a noun in order to avoid a repetition,
f. ex. Tu rencontres Paul? Oui, je **le** rencontre / Do you meet
Paul? Yes, I meet **him**

The reflexive personal pronouns

EX je me lave / I wash myself

subject pronoun	reflexive pronoun	verb
je	me	lave
tu	te	laves
il / elle	**se**	lave
nous	nous	lavons
vous	vous	lavez
ils / elles	**se**	lavent

In French the subject pronoun is always expressed.
'Vous' is used instead of 'tu' as the polite form, f. ex.
Vous cherchez ce livre? Do you search this book?
If a sentence contains masculine and feminine subjects,
the masculine pronoun is used, f. ex.
Où sont les filles et les garçons? **Ils** sont à la maison.
Where are the girls and the boys? They are in the
house.

Personal pronouns: unstressed

EX Je te donne un cadeau / I give you a gift

subject pronoun	dative pronoun	verb
Je	te	donne
Tu	me	donnes
Il	**lui**	donne
Elle	**lui**	donne
Nous	vous	donnons
Vous	nous	donnez
Ils / elles	**leur**	donnent

EX Je te rencontre / I meet you

subject pronoun	accusative pronoun	verb
Je	te	rencontre
Tu	me	rencontres
Il	**la**	rencontre
Elle	**le**	rencontre
Nous	vous	rencontrons
Vous	nous	rencontrez
Ils/elles	**les**	rencontrent

dative pronouns: like reflexive pronouns
exception: 3rd person Sg instead of se: **lui**
         3rd person Pl instead of se: **leur**
accusative pronouns: like dative pronouns
exception: 3rd person Sg instead of lui: **la, le**
         3rd person Pl instead of leur: **les**

Personal pronouns: stressed

EX   Je parle avec toi / I speak with you

subject pronoun	verb	preposition	stressed pronoun
Je	parle	avec	toi
Tu	parles	avec	moi
Il	parle	avec	elle
Elle	parle	avec	**lui**
Nous	parlons	avec	vous
Vous	parlez	avec	nous
Ils	parlent	avec	elles
Elles	parlent	avec	**eux**

OP

The stressed pronoun is used:

after the prepositions, f. ex. Je parle avec **toi**.

in order to show an opposition, f. ex.

lui, il est vieux, **eux**, ils sont jeunes / he is young, they are old

in order to highlight a person, f. ex.

moi, je ne viendrai pas / I, personally, will not come

after the verbe être, f. ex.

Qui est là? C'est **moi**. Who is there? It's me.

in sentences with a comparative, f. ex.

tu es plus grand que **moi** / you're taller than me

in sentences with 'ou' and 'ni':

Qui paie l'addition, **toi** ou **moi**? Ni moi ni toi, chacun paie pour soi.

Who pays the bill, you or me? Neither me nor you, either pays for himself.

The pronoun '**soi**' is used to refer to an indeterminate subject (chacun, personne, on), f. ex.

chacun pense à **soi** / everybody thinks of himself

The pronouns 'y' and 'en'

EX   Does he often think of Paris? Yes, he often thinks of it.
     Il pense souvent à Paris? Oui, il **y** pense souvent.
D   The invariable pronoun ‚y' has the meaning: to that
     thing, to that person.
EX   Does he go to Paris. Yes, he goes there.
     Il va à Paris? Oui, il **y** va.
     He comes from Paris? Yes, he comes from there.
     Il vient de Paris? Oui, il **en** vient.
D   The pronouns 'y' and 'en' can be an adverb of place.

Position of the pronouns

The pronouns are placed before the verb in the following
order:

1	2	3	4	5	6
me					
te	le				
se	la	lui	y	en	verb
nous	les	leur			
vous					

OP

EX   you give it to me / tu me le donne
     I give it to her / je le lui donne
     I meet them there / je les y rencontre
     I speak with them of that / je leur en parle

Elided forms

The elided forms are used before words beginning with a
vowel or silent h. There are elided forms of the following
words: je, me, te, se, le, la and ce, de, ne … (pas), que, si.

41

Adverbs of negation

Ne … **pas** is the usual negation.
The verb is placed between the two parts of the negative,
f. ex.
Je **ne** vois **pas** R / I don't see R
In spoken language ne is often leaved out, f. ex.
Je vois **pas** R.
The auxiliary is placed between the two parts of the
negative, f. ex.
Je **n'ai pas** vu R / I didn't see R
ne … **plus**
Je **ne** vois **plus** R / I never see R any more
ne … **personne**
Je **ne** vois **personne** / I don't see anyone
ne … **rien**
Je **ne** vois **rien** / I don't see anything
ne … **que**.
Je **ne** parle **que** français / I speak only French

OP   Irregular verbs

venir / come
pres.   je viens, nous venons, ils/elles viennent
Pr Pf   je suis venu

vivre / live
pres.   je vis, nous vivons, ils/elles vivent
Pr Pf   j'ai vécu

OP   False friends

achever	finish	*achieve*	atteindre
affluence f	crowd	*affluence*	abondance f
coin m	corner	*coin*	monnaie f

Please learn the words from <u>pasta</u> to <u>shoe</u>.

Eighth day

Arrivée à l'hôtel / Arrival at the hotel

Place: Hotel in Cannes
Tino T, his wife Gina G, their daughter Nora N,
Mr Richard R

T Bonsoir, je m'appelle Tino Baci (boswar shoe mapEl).
   Good evening, my name is Tino Baci. Vous êtes monsieur Richard à qui j'ai téléphoné hier (vusEt moesjoe
   rishar a ki she telephone ijEr)? Are you Mr Richard to
   whom I spoke on the phone yesterday?

R Oui, enchanté (wi ashate). Yes, pleased to meet you.
   Combien de temps restez-vous (kobje doe ta rEstevu)?
   How long are you staying?

T Une semaine (yn soemEn). One week. Nous avons besoin d'une chambre double et d'une chambre individuelle pour notre fille (nusavo boesoe dyn shabr dubl e
   dyn shabr edividyEl pur nOtr fij). We need a double
   room and a single room for our daughter.

R Vous avez de la chance (vusave de la shas). You are
   lucky. Bien que nous avons la pleine saison *il y a* encore
   quelques chambres libres (bje koe nusavo la plEn sEso
   ilja akOr kElkoe shabr libr). Although it is the high
   season *there are* still some free rooms. Il y a deux
   chambres avec salle de bain, balcon et vue sur la mer
   (ilja doe shabr avEk sal doe be balko e vy syr la mEr).
   There are two rooms overlooking the see with a bath-
   room and a balcony.

G Combien coûte une nuit avec petit déjeuner, la demi-
   pension et la pension complète (kobje kut yn nyi avEk
   poeti deshoene la doemipasjo e la pasjo koplEt)? How
   much is it with breakfast, half-board and full board?

R Voici la liste des prix (vwasi la list de pri). This is the

43

price list.

G C'est trop cher (sE tro shEr). That is too expensive. Avez-vous quelque chose *plus bon marché* (ave vu kElkoe <u>sho</u>s ply b*o* marshe)? Do you have anything *cheaper*?

R Nous avons deux chambres avec douche et vue sur les montagnes (nu<u>s</u>avo doe sh*a*br avEk dush e vy syr le m*o*tagn). We have two rooms overlooking the mountains and with shower.

G Est-ce que nous pourrions voir les chambres (Eskoe nu purj*o* vwar le sh*a*br)? Could we see the rooms?

R Volontiers (vOl*o*tje). Of course.
   Après la visite. After the viewing.

G D'accord, nous prenons les chambres (dakOr nu proen*o* le sh*a*br). Okay, we will take the rooms.

R Je vous prie de *remplir* cette fiche (<u>sh</u>oe vu pri doe r*a*plir sEt fish). Would you *fill in* this registration form. Veuillez signer ici (voeje signe isi). Would you sign here.

T *Quelqu'un* peut monter les bagages dans les chambres (kElk*e* poe m*o*te le baga<u>sh</u> d*a* le sh*a*br)? Could *some-body* take the bags up to the rooms?

R J'appelle un garçon (shapEl *e* gars*o*). I will call for a servant. Voici les deux clefs (vwasi le doe kle). These are the two keys.

G À quelle heure servez-vous le petit déjeuner (a kEl OEr sErve vu loe poeti de<u>sh</u>oene)? What time is breakfast served?

R De huit à dix heures (doe yit a dis OEr). From eight to ten.

T Est-ce que vous pourriez nous réveiller à huit heures demain matin (Eskoe vu purje nu reveje a yit OEr doem*e* mat*e*)? Could you wake us at eight tomorrow morning?

R Volontiers (vOl*o*tje). Of course. Voici l'ascenseur (vwasi las*a*sOEr). There is the lift. Bonne nuit (bon nyi)! Good night! À demain (a doem*e*). See you tomorrow.

Après une semaine très belle. After a very good week.

T Pourriez-vous préparer ma note (purjevu prepare ma nOt)? Could you prepare my bill?

R La note est prête (la nOt E prEt). The bill is ready.

T Au revoir, c'était un séjour très agréable (o roevwar setE *e* se<u>sh</u>ur trE<u>s</u>agreabl). Goodbye, we had a very agreeable stay.

G C'était une semaine merveilleuse (setE yn soemEn mErvEjoe<u>s</u>). It was a wonderful week.

N Salut, c'était mega fantastique (saly setE mega *fa*tastik). Bye, it was a mega fantastic stay.

R Ravi d'avoir fait votre connaissance (ravi davwar fE vOtr cOnEs*a*s). It was nice meeting you. J'espère vous revoir l'année prochaine (shEspEr vu revwar lane prOshEn). I hope to see you again next year. Bon retour (b*o* roetur). Have a good journey home!

Possessive adjectives

My father, my mother, my parents
Mon père, **ma** mère, **mes** parents

1 possessor	1 thing / person		several things/ persons
1st pers. Sg	**mon**(m)	**ma**(f)	**mes**
2nd pers. Sg	ton	ta	tes
3rd pers. Sg	son	sa	ses

Our sun, our daughter, our children
Notre fils, **notre** fille, **nos** enfants

several possessors	1 thing/person	several things/persons
1st pers. PL	**notre** (m f)	**nos**
2nd pers. Pl	votre	vos
3rd pers. Pl	leur	leurs

R The possessive adjective agrees in gender with the person or thing 'possessed', f. ex. Elle gare **sa** voiture / she parks her car. Il gare **sa** voiture / he parks his car.
Before feminine words beginning with a vowel or silent h the masculine forms mon, ton, son are used, f. ex.
mon amie / my girlfriend

Relative pronouns

EX Hermann Hesse who is a Nobel prize winner, who everyone knows, reads two poems which I know and which are my favourite poems.
Hermann Hesse qui (1) est un lauréat du Prix Nobel, que (2) tout le monde connait, lit deux poésies, que (3) je connais et qui (4) sont mes poésies préférées.

D There are two relative pronouns:
qui (function: subject); qui can be masculine (1), feminine (4) or neuter, singular (1) or plural (4).
que (function: direct object); que can be masculine (2), feminine (3) or neuter, singular (2) or plural (3).

The interrogative sentence
The interrogative sentence is formed like this:
1. by emphasizing the end of the sentence, f. ex.
Vous lisez **Shakespeare**? Do you read Shakespeare?
2. with the adverb of interrogation est-ce que:
Est-ce que vous lisez Shakespeare?
3. by changing subject and verb:
Lisez-vous Shakespeare?

Demonstrative **adjectives** and *pronouns*

EX Do you meet this boy? No, that.
Tu rencontres **ce** garçon-ci? Non, *celui-là.*
Tu rencontres **cette** fille-ci? Non, *celle-là.*

Pl Tu rencontres **ces** garçons-ci? Non, *ceux-là.*
Tu rencontres **ces** filles-ci? Non, *celles-là.*

D   Demonstrative adjectives are used to designate
persons or things. Demonstrative pronouns represent
a noun.
ci indicates nearness, **là** indicates distance.

R   Before a vowel or silent h ce > cet, f. ex.
cet ami / this friend

OP Irregular verbs

dire / say
pres. je dis, nous disons, vous dites, ils/elles disent
Pr Pf j'ai dit

vouloir / want
pres. je veux, nous voulons, ils/elles veulent
Pr Pf j'ai voulu
conditional: je voudrais

OP False friends

bail m	lease	*bail*	caution f
commander	order	*command*	ordonner
propre	clean, own	*proper*	convenable
store m	blind	*store*	réserve f
contrôler	check	*control*	diriger
fourniture f	supply	*furniture*	meubles m Pl
inconvenant	improper	*inconvenient*	incommode
injure f	insult	*injure*	blesser
lecture f	reading	*lecture*	cours m
librairie f	bookshop	*library*	bibliothèque f
location f	rental	*location*	emplacement
propriété f	property	*propriety*	bienséance f
tentative f	attempt	*tentative*	hésitant

Please learn the words from <u>shop</u> to <u>table</u>.

47

Ninth day

Au restaurant / In the restaurant

Place: Restaurant in Marseille
Gina G, Tino T, Nora N, waitress W

T Bonjour (b*o*sh*ur*). Good afternoon. Désolé d'être en
retard (desole dEtr *a* roetar). Sorry, we are late.

W Cela ne fait rien (soela noe fE rj*e*). It doesn't matter.

T Je m'appelle Tino Baci (shoe mapEl). My name is
Tino Baci. J'ai réservé une table pour trois personnes
dans le coin nonfumateurs (she reserve yn tabl pur trwa
pErsOn d*a* loe ko*e* n*o*fymatEUr). I have reserved a table
for three people in the non smoking area.

W Voici la table (vwasi la tabl). Here is your table.
Asseyez-vous, je vous en prie (asejevu shoe vu*s*apri).
Please take a seat. Voici la liste des boissons (vwasi la
list de bwas*o*). Here is the drink list. Est-ce que vous
voulez un apéritif (Eskoe vu vule *e*naperitif)? Would
you like an aperitif?

G Un kir royal s'il vous plait (*e* kir rwajal silvuplE). A kir
royal please.

N Une boisson sans alcool (*yn bwaso* s*a*salkOl). A soft
drink.

T Un pastis (*e* pastis). A pastis.
Après l'apéritif. After the aperitif.

W Qu'est-ce que vous aimeriez boire (kEskoe vu*s*emerie
bwar)? What would you like to drink?

G Un verre de vin blanc (*e* vEr doe v*e* bl*a*). A glass of
white wine.

N Un jus de fruits (*e* shy doe fryi). A fruit juice.

T Une bière à la pression (yn bjEr a la prEsj*o*). A draught
beer.

W Qu'est-ce que vous voulez comme entrée (kEskoe vu

vule kOm *a*tre)? What would you like as a starter?

T Fruits de mer (fryi doe mEr). Seefood.

N Saumon fumé (som*o* fyme). Smoked salmon.

G Soupe de poissons (sup doe pwas*o*). Fish soup.

W Qu'est-ce que vous voulez manger (kEskoe vu vule ma<u>sh</u>e)? What would you like to eat?

N Je vais prendre un plat végétarien (<u>sh</u>oe vE pr*a*dr *e* pla ve<u>sh</u>etarj*e*). I would like a vegetarian dish. Quel plat vous me conseillez (kEl pla vu moe k*o*sEje)? What do you recommend?

W Pommes de terre avec légume (pOm doe tEr avEk legym). Potatoes with vegetable.

G Je voudrais du poisson (<u>sh</u>oe vudrE dy pwas*o*). I would like fish. Sole avec du riz (sOl avEk dy ri). Sole with rice.

T Je vais prendre le steak et une salade composée (<u>sh</u>oe vE pr*a*dr loe stEk e yn salad k*o*pose). I would like the beefsteak and mixed salad.

W Le steak saignant, à point où bien cuit (loe stEk sEgn*a* a po*e* u bj*e* kyi)? The steak rare, medium or well done?

T À point (a po*e*). Medium.

W Quelle sauce pour la salade (kEl sos pur la salad)? What kind of dressing ?

T Sauce française (sos fr*a*sEs). French dressing.

Après le plat principal. After the main dish.

W Est-ce que vous voulez un dessert (Eskoe vu vule *e* doesEr)? Would you like dessert?

T Quels parfums de glace avez-vous (kEl parf*e* doe glas avevu)? What kind of ice cream do you have?

W Vanille, framboise, fraise, noix et abricot (vanij fr*a*bwas frEs nwa e abriko). Vanilla, raspberries, strawberries, walnut and apricot.

T Une glace mixte et un café au lait (yn glas mikst e *e* kafe o lE). A mixed ice cream and a coffee with milk.

G Quels gâteaux avez-vous (kEl gato avevu)? What kind

of cake do you have?

W Tarte aux fruits, tarte aux pommes et gâteau au fromage blanc (tart o fryi, tarte o pOm e gato o frOma<u>sh</u> bl*a*). Fruitcake, apple cake and cheese cake.

G Une tarte aux pommes, mais avec de la crème Chantilly et un café (yn tart o pOm mE avEk doe la krEm sh*a*tiji e *e* kafe). An apple cake but with whipped cream and a coffee.

N Salade de fruits et un thé citron (salad doe fryi e *e* te sitr*o*). Fruit salad and a tea with lemon.

Après un très bon déjeuner. After an excellent lunch.

W C'était bon (setE b*o*)? Was everything ok?

G C'était excellent (setE EksEl*a*). It was excellent. Faites nos compliments au cuisinier (fEt no k*o*plim*a* o kyisin-je). Would you give our compliments to the chef.

T L'addition, s'il vous plait (ladisj*o* silvuplE). May I have the bill please. Gardez la monnaie (garde la mOnE). Keep the change.

W Merci beaucoup (mErsi boku). Thank you.

The space / l'espace

in the house	á la maison
through the house	à travers (a travEr)
inside ...	à l'intérieur de (*e*terjOEr)
outside ...	hors de (Or)
in front of ...	devant (doev*a*)
behind ...	derrière (dErjEr)
beside ...	à côté de (a kote doe)
on ...	sur (syr)
under ...	sous (su)
over ...	au dessus de (doesy)
opposite ...	en face de (*a* fas)
nearby ...	près de (prE)

The arrival / l'arrivée

I arrived ...	Je suis arrivé ...
seven days ago	il y a sept jours (ilja sEt shur)
last week	la semaine passée (la soemEn pase)
yesterday	hier (ijEr)
today	aujourd'hui (oshurdyi)
a little while ago	il y a peu de temps (ilja poe doe ta)
half an hour ago	il y a une demie heure (doemi OEr)
I have just arrived	je viens d'arriver (shoe vje darive)
I am arriving	je suis en train d'arriver (shoe syi a tre darive)

The departure / le départ

I am going to leave	je vais partir (shoe vE partir)
I will leave ...	je pars ...
immediately	tout de suite (tu doe syit)
soon	bientôt (bjeto)
as soon as possible	le plus tôt possible
in two hours	dans deux heures (da doesOEr)
this morning	ce matin (soe mate)
this afternoon	cet après-midi(sEtaprEmidi)
this evening	ce soir (soe swar)
tomorrow	demain (doeme)

Essential expressions

Pleased to meet you	Enchanté (ashate)
How are you?	Comment allez-vous (kOmatalevu)?
Goodbye	Au revoir (o roevwar)
Say hello to Mrs / Mr	Saluez Madame / Monsieur ... de ma part (salye madame/moesjoe doe ma par)
See you soon	A bientôt (a bjeto)

Do you speak English?	Vous parlez anglais (vu parle *a*glE)?
Does anyone speak English?	Il y a quelqu'un qui parle anglais (ilja kElk*e* ki parl *a*glE)?
Could you help me?	Pourriez-vous m'aider (purjevu mede)?
Could you do me a favour?	Pourriez-vous rendre un service à moi (r*a*dr *e* sErvis a mwa)?
Of course	Naturellement (natyrElm*a*)
Thank you	Merci (mErsi)
That was really kind of you	C'était très aimable de votre part (setE trEsEmabl doe votr par)
You're welcome	De rien (doe rj*e*)
Is there a shop near here?	Est-ce qu'il y a un magasin par ici (Eskilja *e* magas*e* par isi)?
How much is it?	Combien ça coûte (k*o*bj*e* sa kut)?
That is too expensive	C'est trop cher (sE tro shEr)
Do you have anything cheaper?	Vous avez quelque chose plus bon marché (vu̲s̲ave kElkoe s̲h̲os̲ ply b*o* marshe)?
I am afraid I can't come	Je regrette que je ne peux pas venir (s̲h̲oe roegrEt koe s̲h̲oe noe poe pa venir)
Sorry	Pardon (pard*o*)
Don't mention it	Je vous en prie (s̲h̲oe vus̲*a*pri)
Where is the toilet?	Où sont les toilettes?

OP If you haven't understand

I don't understand. Je ne comprends pas (<u>sh</u>oe noe k*o*pr*a* pa). Could you repeat it and speak more slowly? Vous pouvez le répéter et parler plus lentement (vu puve loe repete e parle ply l*a*tm*a*)? Could you write it down for me? Est-ce que vous pouvez me l'écrire (Eskoe vu puve moe lekrir)? Could you translate that for me? Est-ce que vous pourriez traduire cela pour moi (Eskoe vu purje tradyir sela pur mwa)? What is that in French? Comment ça s'appelle en français (kOm*a* sa sapEl *a* fr*a*sE)? How do you pronounce this word? Comment on prononce cette parole (kOm*a* *o* prOn*o*s sEt parOl)?

OP In the supermarket

Can I help you? Je peux vous aider (<u>sh</u>oe poe vu<u>s</u>ede)?
I am just looking, thanks. Non, merci, je ne fais que regarder (n*o* mErsi <u>sh</u>oe noe fE koe roegarde). I like that, I take it. Ça me plait, je le prends (sa moe plE <u>sh</u>oe loe pr*a*). Can I pay by credit card? Est-ce que je peux payer par carte (Eskoe <u>sh</u>oe poe peje par kart)? Could you give me a bag? Pourriez-vous me donner un sac en plastique (purjevu moe dOne *e* sak *a* plastik)?

OP After an accident

There has been an accident. Il y a eu un accident (ilja y *e*n-aksid*a*). Call an ambulance and the police, quick! Appelez tout de suite une ambulance et la police (aple tu doe syit yn *a*byl*a*s e la pOlis)! Could you give me your name, your address and your insurance number. Donnez moi votre nom, votre adresse et le numéro de votre assurance (done mwa vOtr n*o* vOtr adrEs e loe nymero doe vOtr asyr*a*s).

Tenth day

Prepositions of time

EX   Four months ago I hit on the idea of writing a book
      which I have written since 2 months which I have to
      finish in 2 months and which the editor publishes
      in 4 months.

      Il y a 4 mois (1) qu' il me vint l'idée d'écrire un livre
      que j'écris **depuis** 2 mois (2) que je dois achever **en**
      2 mois (3) et que l'éditeur publie **dans** 4 mois (4).

D 1 **il y a**: a time in the past
   2 **depuis**: an unfinished action which has begun in the
      past
   3 **en**: necessary time for the finishing of an action
   4 **dans**: time in the future

à

EX   My aunt lives in Denmark. Her house in the country
      belongs to my uncle.

      Ma tante habite au Danemark (1). Sa maison à la
      campagne (2) est à mon oncle (3).

D·   **à** is used f. ex. before masculine names of countries
      beginning with a consonant (1)
      á indicates f. ex. place (2) possession (3)

de

EX   My friend is arriving from Brussels where yesterday
      from ten to eleven he spokes by heart about the
      European Union.

      Mon ami vient de Bruxelles (1) où hier de dix heures
      à onze heures (2) il a parlé de mémoire (3) de l'Uni-
      on européenne.

D   de indicates f. ex. place (1) time (2) manner (3)

en

EX   My sister lives in France. In summer she goes to
Rome, where she buys a silk shirt.
Ma soeur habite en France (1). En été (2) elle va à
Rome où elle achète une chemise en soie (3).

D   **en** is used:
before feminine names of countries (1)
before months and seasons (2). Exception: au
printemps / in spring
in order to indicate the material (3)

par and pour

EX   One time a week I leave to Nice by love for meeting
a girlfriend; the last week I went by train by Paris
and I read a book written by Victor Hugo.
Une fois **par** semaine (1) je pars **pour** Nice (2) **par**
amour (3) **pour** rencontrer une amie (4); la semaine
passée j'ai voyagé **par** train (5) **par** Paris (6) et j'ai
lit un livre écrit **par** Victor Hugo (7).

D   **par** is used f. ex. in the following cases:
time (1) cause (3) means (5) place (6) agent (7)
pour indicates f. ex. place (2) aim (4)

Please learn the words from <u>take</u> to <u>yesterday</u>.

Le casino / The casino

Monsieur Müller est un joueur passionné. Mr Müller is a passionate gambler. Pour cela il appelle un taxi devant la gare de Naples et dit au chauffeur:

"Al casino, per favore."

Therefore he calls a taxi in front of the Station of Naples and says to the driver: "Al casino, per favore."

Après 5 minutes le chauffeur dit avec un clin d'oeil:

"Voici l'entrée du casino."

After 5 minutes the driver says with a wink:

"There is the entrance to the casino."

À la réception une belle dame est assise qui salue monsieur Müller avec un gentil sourire. At the reception sits a beautiful lady, who greets Mr Müller with a friendly smile.

"Excusez-moi", dit monsieur Müller, "le douanier a dit que mon passeport est périmé."

"Excuse me", says Mr Müller, "the customs officer said, that my passport has expired."

"Ici vous n'avez pas besoin du passeport. Nos clients attachent une grande importance à l'anonymat", dit la dame avec un clin d'oeil.

"Here your passport isn't necessary. Our clients set great store by anonymity ", says the lady with a wink.

"Très gentil de votre part. En Allemagne on doit montrer le passeport chaque fois qu'on va à un casino."

"That's really kind of you. In Germany you must produce your passport every time you go to casino."

"Pour le moment toutes les pièces sont occupées. Mais vous pouvez boire un apéro dans le bar au frais du casino."

"At the moment all the rooms are occupied. But you can drink an aperitif in the bar at the expense of the casino."

Monsieur Müller regarde avec une grande stupeur le profond décolleté de la serveuse à la poitrine généreuse qui dit avec un sourire séduisant:

"Qu'est-ce que vous aimeriez boire?"
Mr Müller looks with great astonishment at the deep décol-
letage of the full-bosomed barmaid, who says with a seduc-
tive smile:
"What would you like to drink?"
Puisqu'il fait très chaud, il répond:
"Un campari avec des glaçons."
Because it's very hot, he answers:
"A campari with ice."
Pendant que la serveuse prépare l'apéritif elle demande:
"Vous êtes d'où?"
Preparing the aperitif the barmaid asks:
"Where do you come from?"
"Je viens d'un petit village près de Baden-Baden en Alle-
magne."
"I am from a little village near Baden-Baden in Germany."
"Qu'est-ce que vous faites dans la vie? What do you do
for a living?"
"Je suis un professeur d'allemand. I am a German tea-
cher."
Le clin d'œil de la serveuse rappelle à monsieur Müller le
clin d'œil du chauffeur et de la dame à la réception. The
winking of the barmaid reminds Mr Müller of the winking
of the driver and the lady at the reception.
"C'est la première fois que vous êtes au casino?"
"Are you in a casino for the first time?"
"Non, à Baden-Baden je vais au casino deux fois par
semaine, le plus souvent toute la nuit; si j'ai commencé une
fois je ne peux plus m'arrêter ."
"No, in Baden-Baden I go to the casino twice a week,
mostly the whole night; when I have begun I cannot stop."
"Ici vous pouvez rester aussi toute la nuit. Quand êtes-
vous allé la première fois au casino?"
"Here you can stay the whole night too. When did you go
to a casino for the first time?"
"Il y a trente ans que nous avons fait le voyage de noces à

Monte-Carlo. Thirty years ago we spent our honeymoon in Monte-Carlo. Pendant que ma femme faisait des achats je suis allé au casino. While my wife went shopping, I went to the casino. La somme minimum était très basse; à combien se monte la somme minimum ici? The minimum stake was very low; what is the minimum stake here?"

"Deux cent Euro. Two hundred Euro."

"Oh, comme c'est haut! Oh, it's very high! À Baden-Baden la somme minimum est seulement deux Euro. In Baden-Baden the minimum stake is only two Euro."

À l'improviste une porte s'ouvre. Suddenly a door opens. Un homme apparaît et derrière lui monsieur Müller voit une fille blonde vêtue seulement avec un slip rouge. A gentleman comes out and behind him Mr Müller sees a blond girl dressed only in some pink pants. Maintenant il comprend, où il se trouve et la signification du clin d'oeil répété trois fois. Now he understands where he is and the meaning of the three winks. Puis il commence à rouspéter. Then he begins to grouse:

"Quel stupide chauffeur de taxi! What a stupid driver! J'ai dit 'al casino, per favore'! I said 'al casino, per favore'!"

La serveuse rit et dit. The barmaid laughs and says:

"Ne le reprochez pas au chauffeur. Don't blame the driver. Vous avez dit 'al casino, per favore'; cette parole signifie en italien une maison, où on s'amuse avec des belles filles. You said 'al casino, per favore'; this word means in Italia a house, where you can have fun with beautiful girls. Une maison où on joue à la roulette s'appelle en italien'casinò'. A house, where you can play roulette is called in Italian 'casinò'

"Un accent faux et ses conséquences", dit en riant monsieur Müller.

"A wrong accent and its consequences", says Mr Müller laughing.

Vocabulary

above all surtout syrtu
accept accepter aksEpte m
accident PH (aksida) m
accompany accompagner
adapter adaptateur (OEr) m
address adresse adrEs f
admission fee prix d'entrée
admit avouer avue
advocate avocat avOka m
afternoon après-midi (aprE)
age âge ash m
air bed matelas pneumatique
air conditioning climatisation
airport aéroport (pOr) m
allergy allergie(alErshi) f
allow permettre (pErmEtr)
alone seul sOEl
already déjà desha
also aussi osi
always toujours tushur
ambulance PH abylas
amount montant mota m
animal PH animal
answer répondre repodr
antique antiquité atikite f
apartment appartement m
aperitif apéritif m
apple pomme pOm f
appointment rendez-vous
apricot abricot
April avril
architecture PH arshitEktyr f
arrival arrivée arive f

arrive arriver arive
art PH ar m
artificial artificiel artifisjEl
artist artiste mf
arm bras bra m
assurance PH asyras f
ashtray cendrier sadrijem
ask demander doemade
~ prier prie
attention PH atasjo f
August août u(t) m
autumn automne otOn m
awake réveiller reveje

B

back dos do m
baggage bagages bagash m Pl
bakery boulangerie bulashri f
balcony balcon balko m
bank banque bak f
banknote billet bijE m
basin lavabo m
bath bain be m
bathrobe peignoir pEgnwar m
battery batterie batri f
bay baie bE f
be être Etr
~ se trouver soe truve
be called s'appeler sapoele
be missing manquer make
beach plage plash f
bed lit li m
beef bœuf boef m
beer bière bjEr f

begin commencer kOm*a*se
beginning début deby m
behind derrière dErjEr
belt ceinture s*e*tyr f
between entre *a*tr
bike bicyclette bisiklEt f
bill addition adisj*o* f
birthday anniversaire m
biscuit PH biskyi
blanket couverture kuvErtyr f
bleed saigner segne
blood sang s*a* m
blue bleu(e) bloe
boat bateau bato m
body corps kOr m
bone os Os m
book livre livr m
bookshop librairie librEri f
border frontière fr*o*tjEr f
born né ne
borrow emprunter *a*pr*e*te
bottle bouteille butEj f
~ of gas bouteille de gaz
box boite bwat f
boy garçon gars*o* m
brake frein fr*e* m
bread pain p*e* m
break casser kase
break-down panne pan f
breakfast petit déjeuner
breathe respirer respire
bridge pont p*o* m
bring apporter apOrte
brochure PH brOshyr
broken cassé(e) kase

broom balai balE m
brother frère frEr m
bucket seau so m
bus PH bys m
~ stop arrêt d'autobus
arE dotobys
butcher boucher bushe m
butter beurre bOEr m
button bouton but*o* m
buy acheter ashte
~ achat asha m
by air mail par avion
C
cable car téléphérique m
cake gâteau gato m
~ shop pâtisserie patisri f
call appeler aple
camera appareil aparEj m
camp camper k*a*pe
can pouvoir puvwar
cancel oblitérer Oblitere
candle bougie bu*s*hi f
car voiture vwatyr f
car hire location de voitures
~ park parc de stationnement
caravan caravane karavan f
carry porter pOrte
case valise valis f
cash desk caisse kEs f
casino PH ca*s*ino m
castle château shato
cathedral cathédrale katedral
cease cesser sEse
cemetery cimetière simtjEr m
centre PH s*a*tr m

60

century siècle sjEkl m

certificate certificat sErtifika

chain chaîne shEn f

<u>chair</u> chaise sh<u>Es</u> f

~ <u>lift</u> télésiège telesjE<u>sh</u> m

<u>change</u> changer sha<u>she</u>

<u>charge</u> taxe taks f

<u>cheap</u> bon marché b*o* marshe

<u>cheese</u> fromage frOma<u>sh</u> m

<u>checkroom</u> consigne k*o*sign f

<u>chicken</u> poulet pulE m

<u>child</u> enfant *afa* m

<u>chocolate</u> chocolat shOkOla

cinema cinéma sinema m

<u>clean</u> nettoyer nEtwaje

~ propre prOpr

clock horloge OrlO<u>sh</u> f

<u>close</u> fermer fErme

cloth tissu tisy m

clothes habits abi m/Pl

<u>coat</u> manteau m*a*to m

<u>code</u> indicatif *e*dikatif m

cloakroom vestiaire vEstjEr

<u>coin</u> pièce de monnaie f

colleague collègue kOlEg m

<u>colour</u> couleur kulEUr f

~ <u>film</u> pellicule couleur f

comb peigne pEgn m

<u>come</u> venir voenir

compartment compartiment

<u>complaint</u> réclamation sj*o* f

concert PH k*o*sEr m

<u>confirm</u> confirmer k*o*firme

congratulations vœux voe

<u>connection</u> correspondance

contain contenir k*o*tnir

contract contrat k*o*tra m

<u>control</u> contrôler k*o*trole

cook cuisiner kyisine

<u>cooked</u> cuit kyi

<u>cost</u> coûter kute

cousin PH kus*e* m

<u>cover</u> couvert kuvEr m

cream crème krEm f

<u>credit card</u> carte de crédit

<u>cross</u> traverser travErse

cross country ski de fonds

cross country ski run

piste de ski de fonds

<u>cup</u> tasse tas f

current courant kur*a* m

<u>cut</u> couper kupe

D

<u>day</u> jour <u>sh</u>ur m

<u>dance</u> danser d*a*se

<u>danger</u> PH d*a*<u>she</u> m

<u>dangerous</u> dangereux(se)

<u>date</u> PH dat f

~ of birth date de naissance

<u>daughter</u> fille fij f

<u>dentist</u> dentiste d*a*tist m f

December décembre s*a*bre m

decision décision desisj*o* f

deep profond prOf*o*

<u>delay</u> retard roetar m

demonstrate démontrer

<u>department store</u>

grand magasin gr*a* maga<u>se</u> m

<u>departure</u> départ depar m

describe décrire dekrir

diesel PH di<u>s</u>El m

different différent difer*a*

difficulty difficulté difikylte f

dinner dîner dine m

direct PH dirEkt

direction PH dirEksj*o* f

dirty sale sal

disappear disparaître (Etr)

discotheque discothèque

discount réduction redyksj*o* f

disturb déranger der*a*<u>s</u>he

diversion déviation deviasj*o*

dive plonger pl*o*<u>s</u>he

do faire fEr

doctor docteur dOktOEr m

dog chien shj*e* m

door porte pOrt f

double room chambre double

dress robe rOb f

drink boire bwar

drinking water eau potable

driving licence permis de conduire

drop goutte gut f

E

each chaque shak

ear oreille OrEj f

Easter Pâques pak f Pl

eat manger m*a*she

economy économie f

egg œuf OEf m

electric électrique elEktrik

embassy ambassade *a*basad f

emergency urgence yr<u>s</u>h*a*s f

~ exit sortie de secours

end fin f*e* f

enough assez ase

entrance entrée *a*tre f

envelope enveloppe *a*vlop f

evening soir swar m

exchange change sh*a*<u>sh</u> m

excuse excuser Ekskys*e*

exhibition exposition (sisj*o*) f

exit sortie sOrti f

explain expliquer Eksplike

express rapide rapid m

eye œil OEj m

F

face visage vis*a*<u>s</u>h m

fair foire fwar f

fall tomber t*o*be

family famille famij f

fashion mode mOd f

fat graisse grEs f

father père pEr m

February février fevrje m

feel sentir s*a*tir

ferry bac bak m

film pellicule pElikyl f

find trouver truve

finger doigt dwa m

finish finir

fire feu foe m

fish pêcher pEshe

~ poisson pwas*o* m

fill out remplir r*a*plir

flat pneu à plat pnoe m

flea market marché aux puces

flight vol m

floor étage eta<u>sh</u> m

flower fleure flEUr f

fog brouillard brujar m
<u>follow</u> suivre syivr
<u>foot</u> pied pje m
<u>forbid</u> interdire *et*Erdir
<u>forget</u> oublier ublie
<u>fork</u> fourchette furshEt f
form forme fOrm f
fortunately heureusement
forward en avant *a* av*a*
<u>fountain</u> fontaine f*ot*e*n* f
France la France fr*a*s f
French français fr*a*sE m
fresco fresque frEsk f
friend ami /e m f
<u>fruit juice</u> jus m de fruit
<u>full</u> plein /e pl*e*
fungus champignon m
funny comique kOmik

G

gain gagner gagne
gallery galerie galri f
<u>garage</u> PH gara<u>sh</u>
<u>garden</u> jardin shard*e* m
gas gaz ga<u>s</u> m
<u>get</u> recevoir roesœvwar
~ procurer prokyre
~ on monter sur m*o*te syr
~ out descendre des*a*dr
~ up se lever soe loeve
gift cadeau kado m
<u>give</u> donner dOne
<u>glass</u> verre vEr m
glasses lunettes lynEt Pl f
glove gant g*a* m
<u>go</u> aller ale
goal but by m

gold or Or m
golf course terrain de golf
go out sortir sOrtir
<u>gram</u> gramme gram m
grandfather grand-père
grandmother grand-mère
<u>grill</u> gril m
<u>group</u> groupe grup m
greet saluer salye
<u>guide</u> PH gid m
<u>guided tour</u> visite guidée

H

<u>hair</u> cheveu shoevoe m
<u>hair dresser</u> coiffeur kwafOEr
<u>half</u> moitié mwatje f
~ demi /e doemi
~ <u>board</u> demi-pension f
<u>ham</u> jambon sh*abo* m
<u>hand</u> main m*e* f
~ bag sac à main
hanky mouchoir mushwar m
happy heureux oeroe
<u>harbour</u> port pOr m
harvest récolte rekOlt f
hat chapeau shapo m
<u>have</u> avoir avwar
<u>have to</u> devoir doevwar
<u>health</u> santé s*a*te f
<u>hear</u> entendre *ata*dr
heat chaleur shalOEr f
<u>heating</u> chauffage shofa<u>sh</u> m
helicopter hélicoptère m
<u>help</u> aider ede
~ aide Ed f
<u>here</u> ici isi
hi salut! saly

63

high season pleine saison f
history histoire istwar f
hold tenir toenir
holiday congé koshe m
~ jour de fête shur doe fEt
holidays vacances vakas f Pl
honey miel mjEl m
horse cheval shoeval m
hospital hôpital Opital m
hotel hôtel otEl m
hour heure OEr f
hours of business heures
d'ouvertures Oer duvErtyr
hunger faim fe f
hurry hâte at f

I

ice-cream glace glas f
~ parlour glacier glasje m
identity card carte f d'identité
ill malade malad
illness maladie maladi f
immediately tout de suite
tu doe syit
important PH epOrta
inclusive compris kopri
infection PH efeksjo f
inform informer eforme
information PH efOrmasjo f
inhabitant habitant abita m
inn auberge obErsh f
inquire demander doemade
insect insecte esEkt m
~ bite piqûre d'insecte pikyr
instead of au lieu de o ljoe
interpreter interprète etrprEt

invite inviter evite
iron repasser roepase
island île il f
Italian italien italje

J

jam confiture kofityr f
January janvier shavje m
jacket veste vEst f
jeweller bijoutier bishutje m
journey voyage vwajash m
juice jus shy m
July juillet shyijE m
June juin shyie m

K

key clef kle f
kilometre kilomètre (mEtr) m
kind gentil shati
kiosk kiosque kjOsk m
kitchen cuisine kyisin f
knee genou shoenu m
knife couteau kuto m
knock frapper frape
know connaître kOnEtr
~ ledge connaissance (nEsas)

L

lady dame dam f
lake lac lak m
lamb agneau agno m
lamp lampe lap f
last durer dyre
laugh rire rir
laxative laxatif laksatif m
leather goods maroquinerie
marOkinri f
leave partir

leg jambe <u>sh</u>a*b* f

<u>lemon</u> citron sitr*o* m

<u>lemonade</u> citronnade Onad f

<u>less</u> moins mo*e*

<u>let</u> laisser lese

<u>letter</u> lettre lEtr f

~ <u>box</u> boite f aux lettres

<u>life</u> vie vi f

~ <u>belt</u> ceinture de sauvetage

~ <u>boat</u> canot de sauvetage

~ guard maître nageur

<u>lift</u> ascenseur as*a*sOEr m

<u>light</u> lumière lymjEr f

~ bulb ampoule *a*pul f

lighter briquet brikE m

lip lèvre lEvr f

~ stick rouge à lèvres ru<u>sh</u>

<u>liqueur</u> PH likOEr f

liquid liquide likid

<u>list</u> liste list f

litre PH litr m

<u>live</u> habiter abite

~ vivre vivr

<u>look</u> regard roegar m

~ regarder roegarder

<u>look for</u> chercher shErshe

<u>lose</u> perdre pErdr

lost property office bureau

des objets trouvés Ob<u>sh</u>E

<u>loud</u> bruyant bryj*a*

love aimer eme

luck fortune fOrtyn f

luckily heureusement ~m*a*

<u>lunch</u> déjeuner de<u>sh</u>OEne m

luxurious luxueux lyksyoe

M

magazine revue roevy f

<u>man</u> homme Om m

<u>map</u> plan de ville pl*a* vil

March mars m

<u>market</u> marché marche m

marvellous magnifique ~fik

match allumette alymEt f

<u>material</u> matériel materjel m

mattress matelas matla m

May mai mE m

meal repas roepa m

<u>mean</u> signifier signifje

measure mesurer moesyre

<u>meat</u> viande vj*a*d f

mechanic mécanicien ~sj*e* m

<u>medical insurance company</u>

assurance f maladie asyr*a*s

<u>medicament</u> médicament m

<u>meet</u> rencontrer r*a*c*o*tre

<u>menu</u> PH moeny m

<u>message</u> PH mEsa<u>sh</u> m

meter mètre mEtr m

<u>middle</u> moyen mwaj*e*

midnight minuit minyi m

<u>milk</u> lait lE m

<u>mineral water</u> eau minérale

miniature golf ~ miniature

minute PH minyt f

mirror miroir mirwar m

mist brume brym f

<u>mistake</u> erreur ErOEr f

mister monsieur moesjoe

mistress madame madam f

mix mélanger mel*a*she

mobile téléphone portable
moment PH mom*a* m
monastery monastère mO~
Monday lundi l*e*di m
money argent ar*sh*a m
month mois mwa m
moon lune lyn f
mooring embarcadère *a*~ f
more plus ply
morning matin mat*e* m
mother mère mEr f
motor moteur mOtOEr m
~ boat canot à moteur
~ bike motocyclette ~siklEt f
~ way autoroute otorut f
mountain montagne m*o*~ f
~ guide guide de montagne
mouth bouche bush f
multi-storey parking couvert
muscle PH myskl m
museum musée myse m
music musique mysik f

N

nail ongle *o*gl m
~ scissors ciseaux à ongles
name nom n*o* m
narrow étroit etrwa
nationality nationalité
nasjOnalite
neck nuque nyk f
necessary nécessaire nesEsEr
need avoir besoin de
avwar boeso*e* doe
never jamais shamE
newspaper journal *sh*urnal m

New Year nouvel an *a*
next prochain prosh*e*
night nuit nyi f
non-alcoholic ~ alcoolisé
noon midi m
nose nez ne m
not ne … pas noe …pa
nothing rien rj*e*
now maintenant m*e*tn*a*
number nombre n*o*br m
nurse infirmière *e*firmjEr f
nut noix nwa f

O

occupy occuper okype
offer offrir Ofrir
office bureau byro m
off season arrière-saison
often souvent suv*a*
oil huile yil f
omelette PH OmelEt f
one on *o*
one way street sens unique
only seulement sOElm*a*
open ouvrir uvrir
~ déboucher debushe
operation opé~ operasj*o* f
opposite en face de *a* fas doe
optician opticien Optisj*e* m
orange PH Or*a*sh f
order commander kOm*a*de
other autre otr

P

paediatrician pédiatre
pediatr m / f
pain douleur dulOEr f

paint peindre p*e*dr
painter peintre p*e*tr m
painting peinture p*e*tyr f
pair paire pEr f
palace palais palE m
paper papier papje m
paraglide parapente ~p*a*t m
parents PH par*a* m Pl
park garer gare
~ parc park m
parking meter parcmètre m
part partie parti f
party fête fEt f
passport passeport paspOr m
pasta pâtes pat f Pl
path sentier s*a*tje m
patience PH pasj*a*s f
patient PH pasj*a*
pay payer peje
~ in verser vErse
pedestrian piéton pjet*o* m
people gens sh*a* m Pl
pepper poivre pwavr m
per cent pour cent pur s*a*
perfume parfum parf*e* m
perhaps peut-être poetEtr
petrol essence es*a*s f
petrol-station station-service
stasj*o* sErvis
pharmacy pharmacie ~si f
phone téléphoner ~fOne
~ téléphone ~fOn m
~ book annuaire du téléphone
anyiEr dy telefOn
~ box cabine téléphonique

phone card télécarte ~kart f
piece pièce pjEs f
pill pilule pilyl f
pillow oreiller Oreje m
pity plaindre pl*e*dr
place lieu ljoe m
plan PH pl*a* m
plane avion avj*o* m
plant plante pl*a*t f
plaster sparadrap ~dra m
plate assiette asjEt f
platform quai ke m
play jouer shue
~ jeu shoe m
pleasant agréable ~abl
please plaire plEr
~ s'il vous plait silvuplE
police PH pOlis f
pocket poche pOsh f
population PH pOpylasj*o*
pork porc pOr m
porter concierge k*o*sjErsh
portion PH pOrsj*o* f
possible PH pOsibl
prefer préférer
present présent pres*a*
press presser prEse
price prix pri m
private privé
profession PH prOfEsj*o* f
programme PH prOgramme
pronounce prononcer ~n*o*se
protect garder garde
protection facture indice de
protection *e*dis prOtEksj*o*

67

pull tirer tire
punctual ponctuel p*o*ktyEl
purification PH pyrifikasj*o* f
purse porte-monnaie
pOrt mOnE m
put mettre mEtr

Q

question PH kEstj*o* f
quiet tranquille tr*a*kil

R

rain pleuvoir ploevwar
~ pluie plyi f
~ coat imperméable *e*pEr~
raw cru kry
razor rasoir ra*s*war m
reach atteindre at*e*dr
read lire lir
ready prêt prE
reception réception ~sEpsj*o*
recommend recommander
roekOm*a*de
red wine vin rouge v*e* ru*sh*
region région re*sh*j*o* f
religion PH roeli*sh*j*o* f
rent louer lue
~ loyer lwaje m
renting location lokasj*o* f
repair réparer repare
~ réparation reparasj*o* f
repeat répéter
report dénoncer den*o*se
reservation réservation sj*o* f
reserve réserver
residence domicile dOmisilm
responsible responsable

restaurant PH rEstOr*a* m
return retourner roeturne
~ retour roetur m
rice riz ri m
ring sonner sOne
river fleuve flOEv m
roast rôti roti m
roll petit pain
room salle sal f
round rond r*o*
rubbish ordures Ordyr f Pl
~ bin poubelle pubEl f
rucksack sac à dos sak a do

S

safe coffre-fort kOfr fOr m
sail faire de la voile vwal
sailing boat bateau à voiles
salad salade salad f
sale soldes sold m Pl
~ vente v*a*t f
salmon saumon som*o* m
salt sel sEl m
same même mEm
sand sable sabl m
sanitary towel serviette
hygiénique sErvjEt i*sh*jEnik
sauce PH sos f
sausage saucisse sosis f
say dire dir
scissors ciseaux si*s*o m Pl
sculptor sculpteur skyltOEr
sculpture PH skyltyr f
sea mer mEr f
~ food fruits de mer fryi
season saison sE*s*o f

seat place plas f
see voir vwar
~ again revoir roevwar
sell vendre vadr
send envoyer avwaje
separate séparé
serve servir sErvir
service PH soevis m
serviette PH sErvjEt f
shadow ombre obr f
shawl écharpe esharp f
sheet drap de lit dra doe li
ship navire navir m
shirt chemise shoemis f
shoe chaussure shosyr f
shop magasin magase m
~ window vitrine vitrin f
shopping centre hypermarché
show montrer motre
shower douche dush f
side dish garniture ~tyr f
sign signer signe
signature PH signatyr f
single seul sOEl
~ room chambre individuelle
shabr edividyEl f
sister sœur sOEr f
sit être assis Etr asi
~ down s'asseoir saswar
size taille taj f
skating patinage patinash m
skewer brochette brOshEt f
ski faire du ski
skiing course cours de ski
skin peau po f

sleep dormir dOrmir
sleeper wagon-lit vagoli
slice tranche trash f
smoke fumer fyme
smoker fumeur fymOEr m
soap savon savo m
sock chaussette chosEt f
socket prise f de courant
pris doe kura
son fils fis m
song chanson shaso f
soon bientôt bjeto
sort sorte sOrt f
soup soupe sup f
speak parler parle
speaker haut - parleur
oparlOEr m
speed vitesse vitEs f
spell épeler epele
spice épice epis f
spicy piquant pika
splendid splendide spladid
spoon cuiller kyijEr f
spring printemps preta m
square place plas
some quelque kElkoe
spend dépenser depase
stairs escalier Eskalje m
stamp timbre tebr m
stand se tenir debout
starter hors d'œuvre
station gare gar f
stay rester rEste
~ séjour seshur m
steak PH stEk m

steal voler vOler
still encore akOr
stomach estomac EstOma m
stop arrêter arEte
~ arrêt arE m
straight ahead tout droit
stranger étranger etrashe m
street rue ry f
stupid stupide stypid
style PH stil m
sugar sucre sykr m
suit complet koplE m
summer été m
sun soleil sOlEj m
Sunday dimanche dimash m
sunshade parasol ~sOl m
suntan cream crème solaire
krEm sOlEr
supermarket supermarché
sypermarshe m
surprise surprendre syrpradr
~ PH syrpris f
swim nager nashe

T
table PH tabl
take prendre pradr
take an interest s'intéresser à
setErEse
take away emporter apOrte
take off décollage ~kOlash m
tax taxe taks f
tea thé m
team équipe ekip f
television télévision ~sjo f
temperature PH taperatyr f

tent tente tat f
terminal terminus tErminys m
terrace terrasse tEras f
that cela soela
thank remercier roemErsje
theatre théâtre teatr m
theft vol vOl m
there là
there and back aller et retour
thermometer thermomètre m
think penser pase
third troisième trwasjEm
thirst soif swaf f
this celui soelyi celle sEl
though bien que bjekoe
Thursday jeudi shoedi m
ticket billet bijE m
~ office vente de billets
tide marée f
low ~ marée basse
high ~ marée hausse
time temps ta m, fois fwa
time table horaire OrEr m
tired fatigué fatige
tobacco tabac taba m
today aujourd'hui oshurdyi
together ensemble asabl
toilet paper papier hygiénique
papje ishienik
toll péage peash m
tomato tomate tOmate
tomorrow demain doeme
tone ton to m
too trop tro
tooth dent da f

toothpaste dentifrice d*a*tifris
to*ù*ch toucher tushe
tour PH tur
tourist office ~ du tourisme
Ofis dy turism
towel serviette de toilette
sErvjEt doe twalet
tower tour tur f
town ville vil f
town hall mairie mEri f
traffic circulation sirkylasj*o* f
train PH tr*e* m
transport PH tr*a*spOr m
translate traduire tradyir
travel voyager vwaja*sh*e
treat traiter trEte
tree arbre arbr m
trolley chariot sharjo m
trousers pantalon p*a*tal*o* m
try essayer esEje
Tuesday mardi m
tyre pneu pnoe m

U

ugly laid lE
umbrella parapluie ~ply m
understand comprendre pr*a*dr
unfortunately malheureuse-
ment maloeroesm*a*
unleaded sans plomb s*a* pl*o*
urgent PH yr*sh*a
use utiliser ytilise

V

valid valable valabl
vanilla vanille vanij f
veal veau vo m

vegetable légume legym m
ventilator ventilateur v*a* m
view vue vy f
village PH vila*sh* m
vinegar vinaigre vinEgr m
visit visiter vi*si*te
visitors tax taxe de séjour
voltage PH vOlta*sh* m

w

wait attendre at*a*dr
waiter serveur sErvOEr m
wall mur myr m
wake réveiller reveje
want vouloir vulwar
wash laver lave
Wednesday mercredi m
week semaine soemEn f
white wine vin blanc v*e* bl*a*
whole tout tu
why pourquoi purkwa
wife épouse epu*s* f
wind vent v*a* m
wine vin v*e* m
winter hiver ivEr m
withdraw retirer roetire
window fenêtre foenEtr f
word mot mo m
woman femme fam f
work fonctionner f*o*ksjOne
~ travailler travaje
working day jour ouvrable

Y

year an *a* m année ane f
yesterday hier ijEr
your ton t*o* m ta f